AGRICULTURAL CONSERVATION: CONVERTING GRASSLAND TO CROPLAND

AGRICULTURAL CONSERVATION: CONVERTING GRASSLAND TO CROPLAND

UNITED STATES GOVERNMENT ACCOUNTABILITY OFFICE (GAO)

Nova Science Publishers, Inc.
New York

For permission to use material from this book please contact us:
Telephone 631-231-7269; Fax 631-231-8175
Web Site: http://www.novapublishers.com

LIBRARY OF CONGRESS CATALOGING-IN-PUBLICATION DATA

Agricultural conservation : converting grassland to cropland / GAO (editor).
p. cm.
ISBN 978-1-60456-630-7 (softcover)
1. Agricultural conservation--Economic aspects--Great Plains. 2. Land use--Economic aspects--Great Plains. 3. Agricultural subsidies--Great Plains--Costs. I. United States. Government Accountability Office.
S604.62.G74A37 2008
333.74'130978--dc22

2008018939

Published by Nova Science Publishers, Inc. ✢ New York

CONTENTS

INTRODUCTION*

WHY GAO DID THIS STUDY

The nation's remaining grassland has several important benefits, such as providing land for grazing and wildlife habitat for many at- risk species. However, over the past 3 centuries about half of the grassland has been converted to other uses, principally cropland. In addition to losing important grassland values, such conversions may result in increased spending on federal farm programs, such as crop insurance, especially in marginal areas. GAO examined (1) the extent of grassland conversions to cropland and the cost of farm program payments for these newly converted cropland acres; (2) the relative importance of farm program payments versus other factors in producers' decisions to convert grassland to cropland; and (3) any impact the Sodbuster conservation provision—which places soil erosion standards on certain converted land—has had on limiting grassland conversions.

WHAT GAO FOUND

No comprehensive and current source of information exists on the conversion of grassland to cropland or on the resulting farm program payments for newly converted land. However, the data that are available show a decline in private grassland nationwide, continuing conversion of native grassland to cropland in some areas of the country, and that certain farm program payments made to producers in South Dakota counties with

---

* Excerpted from CRS Report GAO-07-1054, dated September 2007.

relatively high rates of conversion were significantly higher than payments in other counties. According to USDA's National Resources Inventory, the nation's privately owned grassland decreased by almost 25 million acres between 1982 and 2003. While some conversions are attributable to development and other land uses, the leading type of conversion has been to cropland. Our analysis of South Dakota counties found that between 1997 and 2006, the average annual net crop insurance payment per acre for the 16 counties with the highest rates of conversion was nearly twice as high as the average payment for all other counties in the state.

Farm program payments are an important factor in producers' decisions on whether to convert grassland to cropland. Certainly other factors, including rising crop prices—largely spurred by increased ethanol demand—and the emergence of genetically modified crops and new farming techniques that make cropping on heretofore unsuitable land possible are also important in producers' decisions. Specifically, our analysis found that farm program payments are an important factor in conversions. Several economic studies have reached the same conclusion. For example, a 2006 USDA study found that increases in crop insurance subsidies motivated producers to expand cropland in the contiguous 48 states by an estimated 2.5 million acres in the mid-1990s. Moreover, farm program payments and conservation programs may be working at cross purposes with one another. For example, from 1982 to 1997, 1.69 million acres of cropland in South Dakota were enrolled in the Conservation Reserve Program, while during the same period, 1.82 million acres of grassland in South Dakota were converted to cropland.

The Sodbuster conservation provision has had little impact on conversions. For certain cropland converted from native grassland and classified as highly erodible, Sodbuster requires that producers apply a soil conservation system that does not allow a substantial increase in erosion as a condition to receiving certain farm program payments. However, much of the native grassland converted in recent years is not highly erodible and therefore is not subject to Sodbuster. In addition, according to county-level USDA officials, the cost of controlling soil erosion relative to potential profits from cultivating the land provides little disincentive to conversion. USDA has proposed legislation to make newly converted native grassland ineligible for program benefits.

ABBREVIATIONS

CRP	Conservation Reserve Program
ERS	Economic Research Service
FSA	Farm Service Agency
FWS	U.S. Fish and Wildlife Service
HEL	highly erodible land
NASS	National Agricultural Statistics Service
NRCS	Natural Resources Conservation Service
NRI	National Resources Inventory
RMA	Risk Management Agency
USDA	U.S. Department of Agriculture

September 10, 2007
The Honorable
Tom Harkin
Chairman

Committee on Agriculture, Nutrition, and Forestry
United States Senate

The Honorable
Collin C. Peterson Chairman
Committee on Agriculture
House of Representatives

Before the European settlement of North America, grasslands occupied approximately 1 billion acres of the contiguous United States—about half of the land—mostly west of the Mississippi River. Over the last 3 centuries, about half of this presettlement, or "native," grassland was converted to other uses, and in some states, such as Iowa, almost all the native grassland has been converted. The most common use to which grassland has been converted is cropland for the production of crops such as corn and wheat.[1] This cropland produces food, feed, and fiber—and now, with the rising demand for ethanol and other renewable fuels, energy—and can yield relatively high financial returns to landowners and agricultural producers. However, grassland is also a valuable resource, providing land for livestock grazing; recreational opportunities, such as hunting and fishing; and environmental benefits, such as reducing soil erosion, improving water quality, increasing carbon sequestration, and providing wildlife habitat. In particular, some grassland provides habitat for threatened and endangered and other at-risk species. Converting grassland to cropland reduces or eliminates these benefits, and can result in additional spending on federal farm programs. Wildlife, environmental, and conservation groups, as well as certain cattle industry interests, have expressed concerns that the financial incentives these farm programs provide are a significant factor in landowner decisions to convert grassland to cropland.

The federal farm programs include a variety of income and price support programs for specific commodities, such as corn, soybeans, and wheat; crop insurance; and ad hoc disaster assistance programs. For the purposes of this report, farm program "payments" include commodity-related payments, crop insurance subsidies, and other benefits. The U.S. Department of Agriculture (USDA) administers the farm programs. In recent years, farm program payments have averaged about $20 billion annually.

The conservation compliance provisions of the Food Security Act of 1985, as amended, condition the receipt of farm program payments on a producer's efforts to control soil erosion on highly erodible land and protect wetlands. One of these provisions, known as Sodbuster, requires producers to apply a soil conservation system that does not allow a substantial increase in soil erosion on land converted from native grassland if the land was not cropped before December 23, 1985, and was determined by USDA to be highly erodible land. In addition, USDA conservation programs provide financial incentives for taking conservation actions on working land or for retiring it from production. Several of these programs, including the Grassland Reserve Program and Conservation Reserve Program (CRP), promote the conservation of grassland. Under the Grassland Reserve Program, USDA offers easements and rental agreements to landowners to assist them in protecting, conserving, and restoring eligible grassland—such as important habitat for wildlife. Under CRP, USDA provides about $1.8 billion in annual rental payments to landowners to retire environmentally sensitive cropland from production and establish permanent vegetative cover on this land.

In November 2006, we identified the need for better oversight of farm program payments.[2] We specifically highlighted that USDA support programs may have unintended consequences, including incentives for producers to grow crops on land prone to drought or erosion. Without better oversight to ensure that farm program funds are spent as economically, efficiently, and effectively as possible, we pointed out that USDA has little assurance that these funds benefit the agricultural sector as intended.

In this context, you asked us to determine (1) the extent of grassland conversions to cropland, and the cost of farm program payments related to these newly converted cropland acres; (2) the relative importance of farm program payments versus other factors in producers' decisions to convert grassland to cropland; and (3) any impact the Sodbuster provision has had on limiting grassland conversions.

In conducting our work, we spoke with and reviewed documents provided by officials in USDA headquarters and field locations; the U.S. Fish and Wildlife Service (FWS); farm, wildlife, conservation, and environmental organizations; state governments; and land grant universities. To determine the extent of grassland conversions to cropland, we examined land use data from (1) USDA's National Resources Inventory; (2) USDA's Census of Agriculture; (3) USDA state offices in Montana, North Dakota, and South Dakota; and (4) a collaborative study by Ducks Unlimited, Inc., a private advocacy group supporting the protection and restoration of wetlands and waterfowl habitat, in conjunction with FWS; the South Dakota Department of Game, Fish and Parks; The Nature Conservancy; and the University of Montana. We also reviewed other relevant studies of grassland conversions to cropland. To determine the cost of farm program payments on converted land, we analyzed USDA data on crop insurance and disaster assistance payments. To determine the relative importance of the availability of farm program payments in producers' decisions to convert grassland to cropland, we analyzed payments per cropland acre in counties with relatively high conversion rates of grassland to cropland. We also analyzed farm-level financial information for a South Dakota county that has had numerous conversions. To determine the impact the Sodbuster provision has had on grassland conversions, we examined USDA land use data and conducted interviews with USDA field officials in selected counties with relatively high rates of conversions in Montana, Nebraska, North Dakota, and South Dakota to obtain their views of the impact of Sodbuster on conversion decisions. A more detailed description of our scope and methodology is presented in appendix I. We performed our work between October 2006 and August 2007 in accordance with generally accepted government auditing standards.

Chapter 1

RESULTS IN BRIEF

No comprehensive and current source of information exists on the extent of grassland conversions to cropland or the amount of farm program payments related to this newly converted cropland. As a result, policymakers do not have current information on the extent of conversions for all areas where conversions may have occurred in recent years. Although limited, available data show a decline in private grassland nationwide and continuing conversion of native grassland to cropland in some areas of the country—particularly the Northern Plains—and that these conversions have added to farm program costs. For example, USDA's National Resources Inventory data indicate that the nation's private grassland decreased by almost 25 million acres from 1982 through 2003. While some conversions are attributable to development and other land uses, the leading type of conversion has been to cropland. Our analysis found that crop insurance payments to producers were significantly higher per acre in South Dakota counties with relatively high rates of conversion, adding to program costs. For example, from 1997 through 2006, the 16 South Dakota counties with the highest number of grassland conversions to cropland had an average annual net crop insurance payment of over $13 per acre, while the average payment for all other South Dakota counties was less than $7 per acre. According to USDA officials, this difference may be explained by the fact that the counties with the highest number of conversions are in areas of the state that are more prone to drought and crop losses.

Farm program payments are an important factor in producers' decisions to convert grassland to cropland, but rising crop prices and new farming technologies are also important factors in these conversions. From September 2006 to January 2007, the price of corn increased by over 66 percent, largely because of the growing demand for ethanol, a corn-based renewable fuel. This demand is expected to continue to increase, and corn prices are expected to be relatively high for several years. Genetically modified crops, such as herbicide-resistant soybeans, as well as new farming techniques, such as no-till planting, contribute to conversion decisions as well. These developments have increased the profitability of crop production in some areas that heretofore were considered marginally suitable or generally unsuitable for crop production. Our analysis of the economic effects on a farm, if it were to convert native grassland from grazing to cropping, showed increased income in 3 of the 5 years covered from 2003 through 2007. Without farm program payments, income would have increased only in 1 year. Other studies have confirmed a relationship between farm program payments and conversions. The studies we reviewed generally found that farm program payments provide significant incentive to convert grassland to cropland because they increased the expected profitability of farming while lowering the associated risks. For example, a 2006 USDA study found that increases in crop insurance subsidies motivated producers to expand cropland in the contiguous 48 states by an estimated 2.5 million acres in the mid-1990s. Moreover, farm program payments may work at cross purposes with payments made under conservation programs intended to protect grassland or to convert cropland to grassland or another conserving use. For example, between 1982 and 1997, 1.69 million acres of cropland in South Dakota were enrolled in the CRP, which provides incentives to farmers to convert cropland to grassland, at a cost to the government of about $633 million. However, during the same period, 1.82 million acres of grassland in South Dakota were converted to cropland.

Sodbuster has had little impact on slowing grassland conversions because, in part, much of the converted native grassland in recent years has not been subject to the Sodbuster provision, which applies only to highly erodible land. For example, according to USDA's National Resources Inventory, an estimated 59 percent of the rangeland converted to cropland between 1997 and 2003 in the Northern Plains was classified as non-highly erodible and therefore was not subject to the Sodbuster provision. Similarly, in reviewing records for selected high conversion counties in Nebraska, we found that over half of the land parcels converted from 2003 through 2006 were classified as non-highly erodible. Even when converted grassland is classified as highly erodible and subject to Sodbuster, the potential profits from cropping the land usually outweigh the perceived costs associated with controlling soil erosion. According to USDA officials, the cost of implementing and maintaining the conservation practices needed to comply with Sodbuster's soil erosion control standards generally does little to discourage conversions, especially when the price of corn and other crops is high. Further, these officials said that new technology such as herbicide-resistant crops and no-till planting has reduced the cost of complying with Sodbuster and made farming highly erodible land economically feasible. For the 2007 farm bill, USDA has offered a proposal known as Sod Saver that, according to USDA, would discourage further grassland conversion. In proposing Sod Saver, USDA recognized that properly managed grasslands provide environmental benefits such as the protection of wildlife habitat. Under this proposal, certain grassland—specifically rangeland and native grassland not cropped for the 6 years preceding the effective date of the 2007 farm bill—converted to cropland would be permanently ineligible for farm program payments. The Sod Saver proposal is generally supported by wildlife, environmental, and conservation groups, as well as certain cattle industry interests. However, several farm, crop, and livestock organizations maintain that the proposal would reduce the amount of farmable land available for beginning farmers, and would constrain farmers' ability to adapt to changing market conditions related to the growing demand for crops to produce food and renewable fuels.

In light of these findings, we are recommending that USDA (1) track annually native grassland conversion to cropland to develop a comprehensive and current source of information in those geographic areas where such conversions can occur and (2) study the extent to which farm program payments and conservation programs, such as the CRP, may be working at cross purposes and report its findings to the Secretary of Agriculture and the Congress.

We provided a draft of this report to USDA for review and comment. USDA provided oral comments through the Chief, NRCS, on September 5, 2007, indicating general agreement with the report's findings and recommendations. USDA also said it wanted to ensure that GAO was aware that with few exceptions, the crop insurance program has strict criteria on where converted land may be insured. Although USDA has these criteria, our work found that it does not have a method and the information needed to enforce them. USDA also provided us with suggested technical corrections, which we incorporated into this report as appropriate.

Chapter 2

BACKGROUND

Before the European settlement of North America, grasslands occupied approximately 1 billion acres of the contiguous United States—about half of the land—mostly west of the Mississippi River, as shown in figure 1.

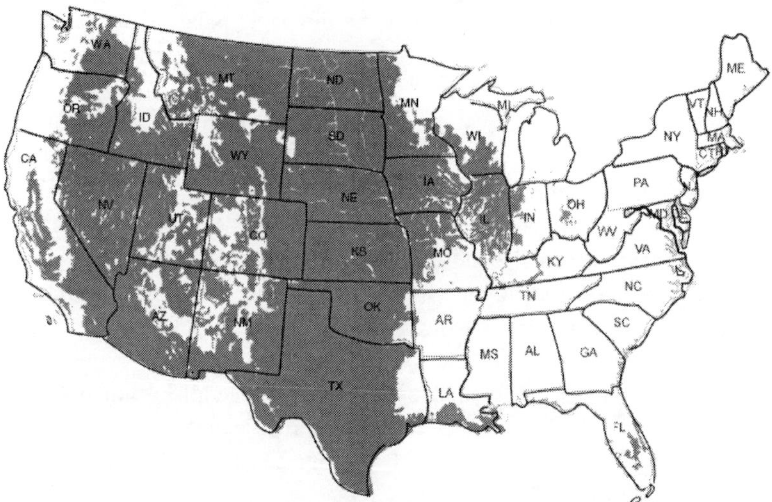

Source: Richard Conner, Andrew Siedl, Larry Van Tassel, and Neill Wilkins. "United States Grasslands and Related Resources: An Economic and Biological Trends Assessment," (2001). http://landinfo.tamu.edu/presentations/grasslands.html (Downloaded January 31, 2007).

Figure 1. U.S. Grasslands before European Settlement.

Over the last 3 centuries, about half of this presettlement, or "native," grassland was converted to other uses, and almost all the native grassland has been converted in some states, such as Iowa and Minnesota. While most of the existing privately owned grasslands are between the Mississippi River and the Rocky Mountains, the grasslands west of the Rocky Mountains are largely under federal management.

The land uses to which native grasslands have been converted include pastureland, developed land, and cropland. Historically, cropland—land used for the production of crops such as corn and wheat—has been the most common use to which native grassland has been converted. Cropland—which produces food, feed, fiber, and now energy, especially ethanol—can yield relatively high financial returns to crop producers and landowners, and these returns generally increase economic activity in rural communities. In 2006, the value of U.S. crop production was $121 billion (43 percent of the value of U.S. agricultural production). As the United States shifts to more renewable fuels, increasing amounts of crops, especially corn, are being used to produce energy. The use of corn to produce ethanol is projected to double between 2006 and 2008 and continue to increase rapidly for several years. Furthermore, crop exports contribute to the U.S. balance of trade. The United States is the world's leading exporter of several major crops including corn, cotton, soybeans, and wheat. Finally, crop production contributes to local economies in rural counties, affecting demand for farm inputs—seed, fertilizer, pesticides, herbicides, farm machinery, and labor—as well as grain marketing and transportation companies.

However, the grassland that cropland displaces also has many economic as well as environmental benefits. Grassland provides forage for grazing livestock; provides recreational opportunities, such as for hunting and fishing; reduces soil erosion; improves water quality; and aids carbon sequestration, which reduces the amount of carbon dioxide, a greenhouse gas, in the atmosphere. Although these benefits generally result from both pastureland and native grassland, those concerned about the continued loss of grassland have placed a very high priority on preserving the remaining native grassland for the following reasons:

- Conservation of native grassland contributes to the maintenance of biological diversity. More specifically, native grassland provides habitat for wildlife and native species, including native grassland bird species, some of which are declining. The conversion of native grassland to other uses, including introduced grasses, can change the structure and function of habitat such that it no longer supports native wildlife species. For example, the loss of native grassland in the Texas coastal prairie eliminated habitat that supported the Attwater's prairie chicken, a federally endangered species native to this area. In addition, research in North Dakota by U. S. Geological Survey wildlife biologists found significantly higher counts of certain grassland bird species in native grassland than in other grassland. Furthermore, the fragmentation of remaining native grasslands may reduce their habitat value and result in them not being large enough to support their natural biodiversity.

- Once converted, restoring native grassland is difficult and expensive, and it is questionable whether native habitat can ever be fully restored. In general, land that is converted back to native grassland does not regain the ecological function of undisturbed native grassland. Furthermore, FWS estimates that the cost of restoring native grassland in eastern South Dakota is about $200 per acre, a substantial amount relative to the 2006 market value of native grassland in that area, which ranged from an average of $751 per acre in northeast South Dakota to $1,055 per acre in east central South Dakota.

Federal farm programs provide payments that can increase the profitability of crop production and may create incentives for conversions. Among these programs are the federal crop insurance program, crop disaster assistance programs, and the marketing assistance loan program.[3]

The federal crop insurance program protects crop producers from production risks associated with adverse weather as well as price risks associated with commodity market fluctuations.[4] USDA's Risk Management Agency (RMA) administers the program in partnership with private insurance companies, which share a percentage of the risk of loss and the opportunity for gain associated with each insurance policy written. RMA pays companies a percentage of the premium on policies sold to cover the administrative costs of selling and servicing these policies. In turn, insurance companies use this money to pay commissions to their agents, who sell the policies, and fees to adjusters when claims are filed. RMA absorbs a large percentage of the crop insurance program's losses—the difference between premiums collected and indemnity payments[5]—and subsidizes a portion of the premium paid by participating producers.

Crop disaster assistance programs—ad hoc programs enacted by the Congress and administered by USDA's Farm Service Agency (FSA)—provide payments to producers to compensate for losses sustained when planting is prevented or crop yields are abnormally low because of adverse weather and related conditions. From 1998 through 2004, ad hoc disaster assistance legislation was enacted and crop disaster assistance payments were made for each crop year. These payments were made to both producers with crop insurance and those without insurance. A May 2007 supplemental spending bill,[6] which authorized crop disaster assistance payments for crop year 2005, 2006, and 2007 losses, prohibited payments to a producer who either waived crop insurance or did not participate in the Noninsured Assistance Program in the year of the loss.

The conservation compliance provisions of the Food Security Act of 1985,[7] as amended, condition the receipt of farm program payments on the producer's efforts to control excessive soil erosion on highly erodible land and protect wetlands. One of these provisions, known as Sodbuster, requires producers to apply a soil conservation system that meets the required level of protection that allows for no substantial increase in soil erosion on land converted from native vegetation if the land was not cropped before December 23, 1985, and is or was determined by USDA to be highly erodible land.[8] A producer applying for certain farm program payments certifies with FSA that he or she will comply with conservation provisions. If the land in question was not cropped before December 23, 1985, and USDA's Natural Resources Conservation Service (NRCS) has not previously determined whether or not the land is highly erodible land, FSA refers the producer's application to NRCS to conduct the determination. If NRCS determines, or has previously determined, that the land is highly erodible, Sodbuster applies and the producer must maintain a conservation system that will not permit a substantial increase in soil erosion. Under NRCS's procedures, this producer must use a conservation system that controls erosion to a greater extent than is required for highly erodible land that was cropped before December 23, 1985.[9] Figure 2 illustrates when a landowner must apply a conservation system, as required by Sodbuster, to control erosion on newly converted cropland.

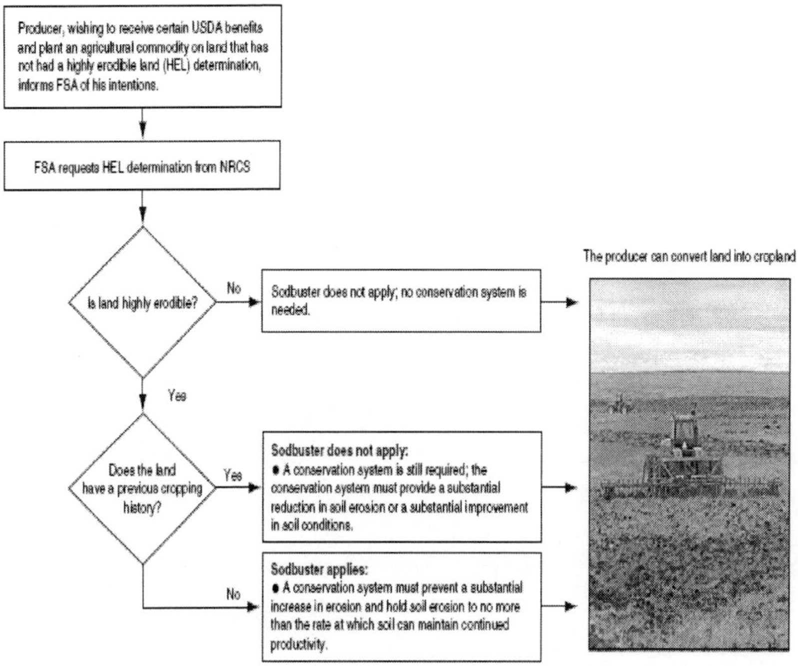

Source: GAO's analysis of USDA's information; photo, U.S. Fish and Wildlife Service.

Figure 2. Process to Determine Sodbuster's Applicability.

Chapter 3

AVAILABLE DATA SHOW CONVERSION OF NATIVE GRASSLAND TO CROPLAND CONTINUES, AND THESE CONVERSIONS ADD TO FARM PROGRAM COSTS

Over the last 25 years, some areas, particularly in the Northern Plains, experienced conversions of native grassland to cropland, and these conversions have added to farm program costs. While there is no comprehensive and current source of information on the extent of native grassland conversions to cropland or the amount of farm program payments made in relation to this newly converted cropland, available sources provide some information on conversions and related costs. Nationwide, total private grassland declined by almost 25 million acres from 1982 through 2003. In addition, conversions of native grassland to cropland continue in the Northern Plains, particularly in areas of North Dakota and South Dakota. Analysis of county-level data indicates that South Dakota counties with relatively high rates of conversions had high crop insurance and crop disaster assistance program costs.

Available Sources of Information Indicate That Grasslands Decreased, and Native Grassland Conversions to Cropland Were Highest in the Northern Plains

Available information on the extent and location of grassland conversions to cropland is not comprehensive and current. For example, data on conversions of grassland to cropland are not available at the state or county level for the most recent years (except in three states—Montana, North Dakota, and South Dakota—where data are being collected on an informal basis to provide information to FWS and Ducks Unlimited on wildlife habitat loss). In addition, the most recent national and regional data are current only through 2003. As a result of these limitations, policymakers do not have current information on the extent of conversions at relevant landscape levels for all areas across the country where conversions may have occurred in recent years. For example, except for the above three states, information is not available on conversions within local areas where further loss of native grassland may affect wildlife populations. Such information—particularly for native grasslands, which are difficult to restore—is important in assessing the need for and the results of policy changes. Moreover, among the available sources of grasslands data, differences in grassland definitions complicate characterization of conversions to cropland and trends in the amount of grasslands. Despite these limitations, available sources provide some information on conversions. Specifically:

NRCS's *National Resources Inventory (NRI)*. The NRI is a periodic statistical survey of land use and natural resource conditions and trends on nonfederal lands.[10] According to the NRI, from 1982 to 2003 in the 48 contiguous states, rangeland and pastureland declined by about 10.4 million acres (about 2.5 percent) and 14.1 million acres (about 10.8 percent), respectively, making the total decline in grassland about 24.5 million acres. Most of the decline in rangeland occurred between 1982 and 1992. These net changes do not indicate the number of acres converted from rangeland and pastureland to cropland. For example, some of the decline in rangeland was due to conversions to non-cropland uses, such as developed land. Appendix II has additional NRI data on net changes in grassland and other land-use categories.

The NRI also provides information on conversions of rangeland and pastureland to cropland. As shown in table 1, for selected USDA crop production regions, the highest conversions of rangeland to cropland were in the Northern Plains, where 2.61 million acres (about 3.5 percent) and 590,000 acres (about 0.8 percent) were converted during 1982 through 1997 and 1997 through 2003, respectively. The annual rangeland conversion rates declined from the 1982 through 1997 time frame to the 1997 through 2003 time frame for each of the three regions that had rangeland. Regarding conversions of pastureland to cropland, the highest amounts were in the Corn Belt, where 4.48 million acres (about 17.6 percent) and 1.66 million acres (about 8 percent) were converted during 1982 through 1997 and 1997 through 2003, respectively.

National Agricultural Statistics Service's (NASS) Census of Agriculture. The Census of Agriculture, conducted every 5 years by NASS, is a census of U.S. farms and ranches and is another source of national data on changes in the amount of private grasslands on farms. The Census of Agriculture does not use the NRI definitions of rangeland and pastureland, and unlike the NRI, the Census of Agriculture combines rangeland and pastureland grasslands into a single category. Also, unlike the NRI, the Census of Agriculture provides data only on net changes and does not provide information on conversions of grassland to cropland. According to the Census of Agriculture, rangeland and pastureland declined by 21.9 million acres (about 5.1 percent) between 1978 and 1992 and 2.9 million acres (about 0.7 percent) between 1997 and 2002. Appendix III provides additional information from the Census of Agriculture on changes in land use for the United States and selected states.

FSA data for Montana, North Dakota, and South Dakota. In recent years, to provide information to FWS and Ducks Unlimited on the amount and location of native grassland converted to cropland, FSA state and county offices in Montana, North Dakota, and South Dakota voluntarily collected county-level data on conversions of grassland that had no prior cropping history.[11] The FSA offices collected this information through existing annual acreage reports. These data showed that within North Dakota and South Dakota, conversions have been highest in counties in the western part of the Prairie Pothole Region, an area of many small, isolated wetlands where the remaining native grassland provides important wildlife habitat. Table 2 shows the available data on acres converted in 2005 and 2006.

Table 1. Conversions of Rangeland and Pastureland to Cropland in Selected Crop Production Regions, 1982-1997 and 1997-2003

acres in millions with margins of error				
Region	Rangeland to cropland, 1982-1997	Rangeland to cropland, 1997-2003	Pastureland to cropland, 1982-1997	Pastureland to cropland, 1997-2003
Northern Plains[a]	2.61	0.59	1.80	0.77
	(2.19-3.03)	(0.47-0.71)	(1.57-2.03)	(0.62-0.92)
Southern Plains[b]	1.17	0.29	0.94	0.42
	(0.98-1.36)	(0.15-0.43)	(0.70-1.18)	(0.28-0.56)
Mountain States[c]	2.04	0.58	0.99	0.80
	(1.63-2.45)	(0.27-0.89)	(0.76-1.22)	(0.55-1.05)
Lake States[d]	d	d	1.98	0.96
			(1.80-2.16)	(0.80-1.12)
Corn Belt[e]	e	e	4.48	1.66
			(4.21-4.75)	(1.46-1.86)

Source: NRCS's NRI data.

Note: These regions have large amounts of cropland and have or previously had large amounts of native grassland as well.

[a] The Northern Plains states are Kansas, Nebraska, North Dakota, and South Dakota.

[b] The Southern Plains states are Oklahoma and Texas.

[c] The Mountain States are Arizona, Colorado, Idaho, Montana, Nevada, New Mexico, Utah, and Wyoming.

[d] The Lake States are Michigan, Minnesota, and Wisconsin. None of these states had measurable rangeland in 1982 or 1997.

[e] The Corn Belt States are Illinois, Indiana, Iowa, Missouri, and Ohio. Among these states, only Missouri had measurable rangeland in 1982 or 1997. Specifically, Missouri had about 143,000 and 88,000 acres of rangeland in 1982 and 1997, respectively.

Table 2. Conversions of Grassland That Had No Prior Cropping History to Cropland in Montana, North Dakota, and South Dakota, 2005 and 2006

in acres		
State	2005	2006
Montana	10,373	6,245
North Dakota	a	20,592
South Dakota	54,404	47,167

Source: GAO's analysis of FSA's data.

[a] According to FSA officials in North Dakota, consistent data are not available for 2005 because county offices did not use consistent data collection methods in that year.

Ducks Unlimited Study.[12] A recent Ducks Unlimited study provided additional information regarding the extent of native grassland conversions to cropland in the western part of the Prairie Pothole Region in North Dakota and South Dakota. The researchers analyzed conversions from 1984 through 2003, examining satellite imagery from this period and performing field checks to identify native grassland. The study found that from 1984 through 2003, an estimated 144,000 acres were converted from native grassland to cropland. The highest conversions were in central South Dakota. The study concluded that the annual conversion rates—which ranged from 0.32 percent to 0.95 percent across the study areas—were relatively low but that the acreage converted was significant from a biological and economic perspective.

Although states other than Montana, North Dakota, and South Dakota may have experienced conversions in recent years, we did not find any other systematic efforts to collect state or local conversions data. However, we were able to obtain some quantitative information that provides some indication of recent conversions in Nebraska. While data on the number of acres converted were not available, NRCS state and county officials in Nebraska provided data for 26 of the state's 93 counties on the number of land tracts on which producers had informed USDA of their intention to convert grassland to cropland.[13] The data show that USDA was informed of nearly 5,200 planned conversions during 2003 through 2006, with the highest county having 678 planned conversions. According to FSA, NRCS, and state wildlife agency officials in Nebraska, many producers were motivated to convert by an interest in gaining irrigation water rights before moratoriums on these rights took effect in certain areas of the state. Some of these officials believe this motivation—and thus the number of conversions—may decline if existing moratoriums on water rights are not modified and new moratoriums are not announced.

Crop Insurance and Crop Disaster Assistance Costs Were Significantly Higher in Counties That Had Higher Conversion Rates

Converting grassland to cropland, and thus bringing more land into production, has the potential to increase government costs because this new cropland is eligible for crop insurance, crop disaster assistance, and marketing assistance loan payments, and could become eligible for direct and countercyclical payments if an update of crop base acres is allowed in the future. However, only limited data are available on government costs associated with grassland converted to cropland because USDA has little information on the location of converted land tracts and generally does not track farm program payments to specific tracts. As such, we analyzed county crop insurance and disaster assistance payments data in relation to 2005 and 2006 data on conversions of grassland to cropland for South Dakota counties.[14] The South Dakota counties that had the most conversions of grassland with no cropping history to cropland also had significantly higher crop insurance and crop disaster assistance costs than other counties. Specifically, we found:

Crop insurance. Our analysis of RMA's crop insurance data indicates that conversions of grassland with no cropping history added disproportionately to government costs for crop insurance in South Dakota. Table 3 shows the net crop insurance payments received by producers in the 16 South Dakota counties with the highest rates of conversions in 2005 and 2006 in comparison with the net payments received by producers in the state's other counties. The 16 highest conversion counties had net crop insurance payments that averaged $13.03 per acre from 1997 to 2006, almost twice as much as the $6.66 per acre net payment received in South Dakota's remaining 50 counties. Also illustrated in the table is the contrast between the net payments in the 16 highest conversion counties and 7 historically cropped counties in southeast South Dakota that had a negative net crop insurance benefit during this period—that is, crop producers in these counties collectively paid more into the crop insurance program as premiums and other fees than they received from the program as indemnity payments.[15]

Table 3. Comparison of Net Crop Insurance Payments in South Dakota for the 16 Highest Conversion Counties versus Other Counties

Area	Crop	Crop years 1997 to 2006		Crop years 1989 to 2006	
		Total	Per acre	Total	Per acre
16 counties with the highest conversions	Corn	$255,520,183	$22.78	$280,392,006	$18.62
	All crops[a]	485,522,546	13.03	550,751,456	10.30
50 other counties	Corn	231,662,594	8.27	290,214,231	7.11
	All crops[a]	532,176,375	6.66	672,826,085	5.67
7 selected historically cropped counties[b]	Corn	(3,562,466)	(0.45)	5,135,553	0.42
	All crops[a]	(3,059,947)	(0.19)	11,805,739	0.49
State totals	Corn	$487,182,777	$12.42	$570,606,237	$10.21
	All crops[a]	$1,017,698,921	$8.68	$1,223,577,541	$7.11

Source: GAO's analysis of RMA's data.

Note: Net crop insurance payments are the indemnity payments that producers received less the premiums and administrative fees that producers pay. We did not include government costs resulting from (1) payments to insurance companies for underwriting gains and administrative and overhead expenses and (2) the cost of RMA operating expenses in this analysis because county-level data on these costs were not available.

[a] Includes all crops except forage production and forage seeding.

[b] These counties have not had large increases in crop production in recent years and are located in two adjacent NRCS major land resource areas.

Crop disaster assistance payments. Similar to our crop insurance analysis, our analysis of FSA crop disaster assistance payments data indicates that conversions of grassland with no cropping history add disproportionately to government costs for disaster assistance payments in South Dakota.[16] Table 4 shows the crop disaster assistance payments received by producers in the 16 South Dakota counties with the highest conversion rates in comparison with the payments received by producers in other South Dakota counties. From 1998 to 2004, crop disaster assistance payments in the 16 highest conversion counties totaled more than $195 million (40 percent of the state total), compared with approximately $292 million for the other 50 South Dakota counties, including about $16 million in 7 historically cropped counties in southeast South Dakota.

Table 4. Comparison of Crop Disaster Assistance Payments in South Dakota for the 16 Highest Conversion Counties Versus Other Counties

Crop years	16 counties with the highest conversions (as a percentage of state totals)	All 50 other counties	7 selected historically cropped counties[a]	State totals
1998	$8,534,884 (38%)	$13,710,472	$393,778	$22,245,356
1999	16,063,451 (40%)	24,502,868	4,969,368	40,566,319
2000	23,266,266 (45%)	28,741,631	1,992,956	52,007,897
2001	12,480,417 (34%)	24,474,570	2,782,104	36,954,987
2002	74,432,452 (42%)	104,322,913	2,716,984	178,755,365
2003	43,800,987 (46%)	50,521,907	2,796,699	94,322,894
2004	16,744,315 (27%)	45,360,495	784,346	62,104,810
Total	$195,322,772 (40%)	$291,634,856	$16,436,235	$486,957,628

Source: GAO's analysis of FSA's data.

Notes: (1) These crop disaster assistance payments include payments for losses of major cultivated crops, such as corn, soybeans, and wheat, as well as fruits and vegetables, such as melons, apples, cabbage, and beets. In addition, some payments were made for grass losses. However, according to an FSA official, these payments were not for grazing losses. (2) In analyzing crop disaster assistance payments, we did not calculate payments per acre because data on the number of acres that potentially were eligible for these payments were not available.

[a] These counties have not had large increases in crop production in recent years and are located in two adjacent NRCS major land resource areas.

According to USDA officials, a possible reason for the relatively high crop insurance and disaster assistance payments in South Dakota counties with the highest conversion rates is that these counties are in areas that are more prone to drought and crop losses than other major crop-producing counties. Drought has been the largest cause of crop insurance indemnity payments nationwide from 1989 to 2004, accounting for about 40 percent of the primary causes of total indemnity payments.

Our 2005 report on crop insurance explains why areas that are prone to frequent or severe crop losses may have relatively high crop insurance costs.[17] The crop insurance program has high premium subsidies to encourage participation. Premium subsidies are calculated as a percentage of the total premium and can be as high as 67 percent. The subsidies shield producers from the full cost of growing crops in these areas. Because

premiums are higher in areas that are prone to frequent or severe crop losses than in the major crop-producing counties, premium subsidies have the effect of causing crop insurance costs to be higher in these areas.

Chapter 4

Farm Program Payments, Rising Crop Prices, and the Adoption of New Farming Technologies Provide Incentives to Expand Crop Production on Native Grasslands

Federal farm program payments are an important factor in producers' decisions to convert native grassland to cropland, but rising crop prices and advances in crop production technology are also important factors in these conversions. Specifically, increased crop prices, due largely to rising ethanol demand, are important in producers' decisions. In addition, the adoption of genetically modified crops as well as new farming techniques have made cropping more profitable on land previously considered to be marginally suitable or generally unsuitable for crop production. Regarding farm program payments, our analysis of crop production costs and returns and our review of economic studies indicate that these payments are an important factor in producers' conversion decisions. Moreover, the incentives farm programs provide to convert grassland to cropland appear to be inconsistent with USDA conservation programs that encourage producers to either maintain grassland or convert cropland to grassland or another conserving use.

Rising Crop Prices and Advanced Crop Production Technologies Are Important Factors in Decisions to Convert Native Grassland to Cropland

Increasing demand for crops used to produce ethanol and other renewable fuels has caused crop prices to increase, increasing the profitability of crop production and providing incentives for conversions. For example, the price of a March 2007 corn futures contract on the Chicago Board of Trade rose from $2.50 per bushel in September 2006 to $4.16 per bushel in January 2007, an increase of more than 66 percent. A May 2007 USDA study stated that the increased demand for renewable fuels would result in continued expansion of crop acreage and bring new land into crop production, particularly in the Corn Belt and the Northern Plains.[18] Furthermore, a June 2007 NASS report announced that corn growers had planted 92.9 million acres of corn in 2007, 14.6 million acres more than were planted in 2006 and the highest total since 1944.[19] NASS stated that this increased corn acreage was partially offset by reduced soybean acreage in the plains and the Corn Belt. USDA and agricultural experts expect this demand to continue to increase, and corn and other crop prices are expected to be relatively high for several years. NRCS and FSA officials in states and counties with the highest conversions of grassland to cropland confirmed that crop prices strongly influence producers' conversion decisions.

In addition, the availability of advanced crop production technologies, including genetically modified crops, such as herbicide-resistant soybeans, and new farming techniques, such as no-till planting, contribute to producers' decisions to convert native grassland to cropland. For example, herbicide-resistant soybeans became available to farmers for the first time in 1996, and, according to USDA, usage nationwide expanded to over 40 percent of soybean acreage in 1998 and then to 87 percent by 2005 (95 percent in South Dakota). The use of these soybean varieties makes weed control easier and has, in turn, made no-till planting—a conservation practice that reduces soil erosion and conserves moisture while also cutting fuel and labor costs—more feasible. These developments have reduced the cost of production and made it more profitable to produce high-value crops, especially corn and soybeans, in some areas that historically were considered marginally suitable or generally unsuitable for crop production. FSA and NRCS officials confirmed that advanced crop production technologies strongly influence producers' conversion decisions.

FARM PROGRAM PAYMENTS PROVIDE INCENTIVES TO CONVERT NATIVE GRASSLAND TO CROPLAND BY INCREASING PRODUCERS' INCOME AND REDUCING THEIR FINANCIAL RISKS

Farm program payments, including crop insurance, crop disaster assistance, and marketing assistance loan payments, are important factors in producers' decisions to convert native grassland to cropland because they reduce producers' financial risks and, in many cases, increase producers' profits over maintaining grassland. To evaluate the impact of farm program payments and other factors in producers' conversion decisions, we prepared a partial budget analysis for a hypothetical 160-acre tract in a South Dakota county—located in the Prairie Pothole Region—that was among the state's highest counties in conversions of grassland that had no cropping history in 2005 and 2006. A partial budget analysis evaluates the economic effects of making an adjustment to part of the farm operation, such as changing what is produced or buying new machinery. Specifically, we compared the estimated costs and returns for 2003 through 2007 from 160 acres of native grassland—used for grazing as part of a cow-calf operation—to the costs and returns if the same land had been converted to cropland in 2003 and used to produce corn, soybeans, and spring wheat through 2007. This period exhibited a variety of yield and price scenarios as well as farm program payments and thus may illustrate how the significance of farm program payments can change from year to year.

We found that for certain years, high crop prices as well as farm program payments would provide economic incentives for a producer to convert native grassland used for grazing in a cow-calf operation to a cropping operation. In 3 of the 5 years, the conversion from grazing to cropping would have resulted in increased income. In the other 2 years, the conversion would have resulted in reduced income largely because cattle prices were high relative to crop prices and farm program payments were lower than in the other years. Without any farm program payments, income would have increased only in 2007, but in view of projections that crop prices will remain relatively high, this increase in income without farm program payments may continue for several years.[20] However, even with high crop prices, farm program payments from crop insurance and crop disaster assistance likely will continue to be a relevant factor in conversion decisions because of the need for protection against adverse crop production risks, such as drought. Table 5 shows the net change in income from shifting to crop production from a cow-calf operation on a 160-acre parcel of land, with and without farm program payments (crop insurance, crop disaster assistance, and marketing assistance loan payments).[21] The table also shows corn prices and yields as well as calf and cow prices during this period.

We did not attempt to evaluate the social, environmental, and wildlife habitat costs and benefits of this conversion. Furthermore, although crop prices are projected to continue to rise over the next several years, the likelihood of prices remaining at such high levels, especially in conjunction with high levels of production, may not materialize. In the absence of data on future weather patterns, yields, and commodity prices, we did not project future rates of return. Moreover, we did not project future rates of conversion because we cannot speculate on many of the factors that enter into producers' land use decisions, such as their aversion to risk in the presence of significant potential crop yield variability, although the stabilizing effect of crop insurance would tend to lessen risk concerns, especially compared to livestock grazing. Nevertheless, this analysis demonstrates that there have been economic incentives for producers, at least in the short run, to shift into crop production on native grassland. It also illustrates the importance of farm program payments in years of lower crop prices or yields. Appendix IV provides more information on our partial budget analysis.

In addition to our partial budget analysis, several economic studies we reviewed found that farm program payments influence producers' conversion decisions because they increase the expected profitability of cropping land while lowering the risks. For example, a study by USDA's Economic Research Service (ERS) found that increased crop insurance subsidies in the mid-1990s encouraged producers to expand crop production in the contiguous 48 states by an estimated 2.5 million acres, with most of the land coming from pastureland and other grassland. Another recent paper, by Iowa State University agricultural economists, concluded that the reduction in risk by crop insurance and commodity programs creates incentives for farmers and landlords to focus on growing the commodities supported by these programs. In addition, some of the economic studies we reviewed raised the possibility that land value appreciation due to farm program payments may be another economic incentive for farmers to convert native grassland to cropland. Since the value of agricultural land depends, in part, upon expected future earnings from farming, purchasers of land will pay a higher price for land that is expected to provide a future stream of farm program payments. For example, ERS reported that the effect of farm program payments on land values varies widely throughout the United States but that increases are highest in the Northern Plains. For more detailed summaries of these and other studies that we examined, see appendix V.

Most of the FSA and NRCS state and local officials in Montana, Nebraska, North Dakota, and South Dakota confirmed that farm program payments, specifically crop insurance, crop disaster assistance, and marketing assistance loan payments are important—although not always the most important—factors in producers' conversion decisions. In particular, among the farm programs, the officials noted the importance of crop insurance because it reduces the risk of growing crops. Nearly all of these officials believed that farm program payments play a greater role in producer decisions when crop prices are lower. For example, several officials noted that a reduction in program payments would have had a more pronounced effect in reducing crop conversions 2 years ago, before the prospect of increased demand for ethanol contributed to higher corn prices.

INCENTIVES TO CONVERT GRASSLAND MAY WORK AT CROSS PURPOSES WITH USDA CONSERVATION PROGRAMS

The incentives provided by farm program payments appear to be inconsistent with USDA conservation programs, such as the Wetlands Reserve Program,[22] the Grassland Reserve Program,[23] and CRP. These conservation programs, among other things, pay producers and landowners to either maintain grassland or convert cropland to grassland or another conserving use. However, these programs appear to be at odds with farm programs that provide incentives for conversions of grassland to cropland. For example, NRI data on South Dakota CRP enrollments—which represent conversions of cropland to grassland—and conversions of grassland to cropland illustrate this apparent inconsistency. From 1982 through 1997, 1.69 million acres of cropland in South Dakota were enrolled in CRP—with almost all of this acreage planted in grasses—at a total government cost of about $633 million. However, during the same period, 1.82 million acres of grassland in South Dakota were converted to cropland. About half of this acreage had been rangeland, generally supporting native grasses and vegetation, and the other half pastureland. Other states had similar patterns during this period. For example, North Dakota had CRP enrollments of 2.8 million acres, CRP costs of about $973 million, and grassland conversions to cropland of 1.16 million acres. Montana had CRP enrollments of 2.7 million acres, CRP costs of about $957 million, and conversions to cropland of 1.35 million acres.

Table 5. Estimated Net Change in Income for a Shift to Crop Production from a Cow-Calf Grazing Operation on a 160-Acre Tract in Central South Dakota, 2003-2007

Factors	2003	2004	2005	2006	2007
Net change in income[a]					
With farm program payments (crop insurance, crop disaster assistance, and marketing assistance loan payments)	$3,761.20	($3,602.75)	($4,834.66)	$2,366.35	$2,099.47
Without farm program payments (crop insurance, crop disaster assistance, and marketing assistance loan payments)	($8,499.29)	($6,631.58)	($7,634.62)	($6,729.35)	$2,099.47
Selected prices and yields					
Corn price ($ per bushel)[b]	$2.36	$1.64	$1.76	$3.37	$3.52
Corn yield (bushels per acre)[c]	37.1	84.4	81.2	41.5	69.0
Calf price ($ per 100 pounds)[d]	$111.38	$121.59	$136.85	$113.16	$124.48
Cow price ($ per head)[e]	$616.50	$750.83	$839.27	$797.55	$769.00

Source: GAO's analysis using data from South Dakota State University, NRCS, NASS, RMA, FSA, and Drovers' Inc.

Notes: (1) We assumed a decision was made to convert to crop production in 2003 and carried forward through 2007. (2) The net change in income is the result of comparing the alternate income streams from cropping (corn, soybeans, and spring wheat) versus grazing (cow-calf operation). (3) Both herd liquidation and conversion costs were amortized over a 5-year period from 2003 to 2007 at a 6 percent rate of interest.

[a] While the 2003 to 2006 results are retrospective, the 2007 crop had not been harvested as of July 2007. On the basis of July 2007 crop prices and USDA estimates, we assumed no marketing assistance loan payments would be made for 2007. We did not include any crop insurance or disaster assistance payments for 2007, although such payments may be made in the future.

[b] Corn prices for 2003 through 2006 are yearly averages of weekly cash prices in central South Dakota from the South Dakota State University extension grain marketing service. Corn prices for 2007 are average weekly cash prices for the Central South Dakota region from January to July 2007, from South Dakota State University extension service.

[c] Corn yields for 2007 are a moving average of NASS county yields, adjusted for soil productivity.

[d] For 2003 through 2006, calf prices are November South Dakota stocker cattle prices, monthly average, obtained from South Dakota State University's "Cattle Market Review," June 22, 2007, for 500 to 600 pound steers. For 2007, calf prices are average monthly prices for the first 6 months of 2007, January through June.

[e] Cow prices are bred female prices for "young and middle aged" bred cows from the central region of the United States which includes South Dakota, obtained from Drovers. For 2007, bred female prices are average monthly prices for the first 5 months of 2007, January through May.

Chapter 5

SODBUSTER HAS HAD LITTLE IMPACT ON NATIVE GRASSLAND CONVERSIONS

Sodbuster has had little impact in limiting the conversion of native grassland to cropland, in part because much of the native grassland converted in recent years is not highly erodible and therefore not subject to Sodbuster. According to USDA officials, even in most cases where Sodbuster applies, the costs associated with Sodbuster compliance have not been enough to deter producers from converting the land. USDA and some stakeholder organizations have suggested a proposal known as Sod Saver that would discourage native grassland conversions by making converted land ineligible for farm program payments.

MUCH OF THE NATIVE GRASSLAND CONVERTED IN RECENT YEARS WAS NOT SUBJECT TO SODBUSTER

Much of the native grassland converted to cropland in recent years is classified as non-highly erodible land and thus is not subject to Sodbuster. NRI data on the percentage of rangeland converted to cropland and classified as highly erodible provide an approximation of the percentage of conversions that are subject to Sodbuster. According to NRI data, between 1997 and 2003, an estimated 59 percent of the rangeland converted to cropland in the Northern Plains production region—encompassing Kansas, Nebraska, North Dakota, and South Dakota—was classified as non-highly erodible. In the Southern Plains and the Mountain regions, which also have large amounts of rangeland, NRI data for this period indicate an estimated 43 percent and 47 percent, respectively, of the rangeland acres that producers converted were classified as non-highly erodible. In addition, according to our analysis of NRCS records for selected Nebraska counties that have had relatively high conversion rates, slightly over half of the land parcels converted in those counties between 2003 and 2006 were classified as non-highly erodible. Because non-highly erodible land is not subject to Sodbuster, producers who convert such land do not have to bear the cost of applying conservation systems in order to maintain farm program benefits.

EVEN WHEN PLANNED CONVERSIONS ARE SUBJECT TO SODBUSTER, PRODUCERS ARE NOT USUALLY DETERRED

According to FSA and NRCS officials, even when native grassland that is to be converted is classified as highly erodible, producers generally perceive that the potential profits from cropping the land outweigh the potential costs of controlling soil erosion as required by Sodbuster. As such, officials in Montana, Nebraska, North Dakota, and South Dakota counties that have had relatively high conversion rates said that the costs associated with meeting Sodbuster's soil erosion standards usually do not discourage native grassland conversion, especially when crop prices are high and crop production is profitable. Specifically, these officials said Sodbuster rarely or never deterred conversions. According to these officials, the cost of complying with Sodbuster has been reduced by new crop production technologies. For example, almost all of the officials cited no-till planting as a low-cost management practice that controls soil erosion sufficiently to meet Sodbuster requirements and added that the development of herbicide-resistant crops has facilitated producers' adoption of no-till planting by making it easier to control weeds without using tillage.

The views expressed by the officials we spoke with are generally consistent with the responses of local NRCS officials to our 2002 survey, in which we asked them to rate the effectiveness of Sodbuster in limiting the conversion of native grassland.[24] The survey results for four states with relatively high rates of conversions—Montana, Nebraska, North Dakota, and South Dakota—are shown in table 6. As indicated in the table, the majority of officials in three of these states—Montana, Nebraska, and South Dakota—responded that Sodbuster was slightly or not effective in limiting native grassland conversion. Nearly 44 percent of officials in North Dakota provided a similar response.

Table 6. Local NRCS Officials' Responses to GAO Survey Question on the Effectiveness of Sodbuster in Limiting the Conversion of Native Grassland to Cropland

	percent				
State	Extremely effective	Very effective	Moderately effective	Somewhat effective	Slightly or not effective
Montana	0	11.9	7.1	28.6	52.4
Nebraska	0	4.1	11.0	15.1	69.9
North Dakota	0	16.7	18.8	20.8	43.8
South Dakota	1.9	7.7	13.5	17.3	59.6

Source: GAO survey results.

USDA and Some Stakeholder Organizations Have Offered a Proposal to Discourage Grassland Conversions

To discourage future conversions, USDA and some stakeholder organizations have suggested a proposal known as Sod Saver that would make certain grassland—primarily native grassland—ineligible for farm program payments if it is converted to cropland. USDA's proposed legislative language—issued in April 2007—applies to rangeland and native grassland not used for crop production at any time during the previous 6 years preceding the effective date of the 2007 farm bill. If such land is converted to crop production, it would be permanently ineligible for a wide range of farm program payments, including direct and countercyclical, marketing assistance loan, conservation, disaster assistance, and crop insurance payments. According to USDA's proposal, Sod Saver is needed because, among other things, grasslands provide important ecological functions and the rate of conversion to cropland could increase greatly over the next several years as increased production of biofuels boosts the demand for corn and other crops.

Most NRCS state and local officials we spoke with suggested that barring newly converted cropland from farm program payments, as called for under Sod Saver, would be a deterrent to new conversions in their counties. However, FSA state and local officials we interviewed were less certain than the NRCS officials about Sod Saver's potential impact. While generally acknowledging that barring farm program payments would affect some conversion decisions, these officials placed more emphasis on the impact of crop prices and advanced production technologies. Officials from both agencies agreed that Sod Saver's impact would be less when crop prices are high than when they are low.

Certain farm, crop, and livestock organizations have expressed opposition to USDA's Sod Saver proposal. These organizations include the American Farm Bureau Federation, National Association of Wheat Growers, National Corn Association, National Cotton Council, National Pork Producers Council, United Egg Producers, and USA Rice Federation. For example, a crop organization official we interviewed said that advances in crop production technology continue to make more land suitable for cropping and that it would be inequitable for some crop producers to receive farm program payments on their cropland while others could not. In a May 15, 2007, letter, organizations opposed to the Sod Saver proposal expressed their concerns. Among other things, they said

- Sod Saver would constrain farmers' ability to adapt to changing market conditions related to the growing demand for crops to produce food and renewable fuels.
- Sod Saver would reduce the amount of farmable land available for beginning farmers.
- Current information on the extent of conversions is insufficient to justify the Sod Saver proposal.
- Existing policy—referring to the current conservation compliance provisions, including Sodbuster—is effectively controlling soil erosion on highly erodible land.

On the other hand, the Sod Saver approach is supported by a number of wildlife, environmental, and conservation organizations, as well as certain cattle industry interests. These organizations include, Ducks Unlimited, Pheasants Forever, the North Dakota and South Dakota chapters of the Wildlife Society, and the South Dakota Cattlemen's Association. In particular, wildlife organizations have emphasized that Sod Saver would help maintain native grassland habitat that is important for waterfowl and grassland birds, especially in Prairie Pothole Region areas of Montana, North Dakota, and South Dakota. In addition, a cattle industry official we spoke with expressed concern that farm program payments encourage conversions and subsidize crop production, putting cattle producers at a disadvantage relative to crop producers in the competition for land. In a May 29, 2007, letter, a coalition of representatives from Montana, North Dakota, and South Dakota wildlife organizations and agencies responded to arguments against the Sod Saver proposal. Among other things, they said

- Sod Saver would not prevent farmers from responding to market signals because it would allow conversions to cropland.
- Beginning farmers would not have good prospects for success if they grew crops on marginal lands that have not been cropped previously, and beginning ranchers would benefit from Sod Saver because it would result in more grassland being available to them.
- Available FSA and NRCS data and anecdotal information about conversions are sufficient to justify the Sod Saver proposal.
- Soil erosion is still a significant problem in North Dakota and South Dakota, and the conservation compliance provisions, including Sodbuster, do not prevent the conversion of native grassland to cropland.

Chapter 6

CONCLUSIONS

In the absence of more comprehensive and current data, policymakers and stakeholders cannot fully understand the extent of conversions of native grassland to cropland or how farm program payments and other factors influence producers' conversion decisions. More complete information, especially at the county or local level, would enable stakeholders to identify where conversions are occurring and the environmental implications. In addition, having this information would be a first step in assessing the additional farm program costs that result from conversions. Such knowledge can help in developing policies balancing the environmental and economic benefits of grasslands against the rising demand for food, feed, fiber, and fuel from renewable sources. In developing the means to collect such information, USDA could draw on the experiences of FSA state and county offices in Montana, North Dakota, and South Dakota, which have incorporated the collection of conversions data into their annual acreage reporting process. In addition, the dynamic between USDA farm program payments and conservation programs needs to be better understood. Available data suggest that USDA's programs that increase the profitability of cropping and its programs that encourage conservation of rural land may be working at cross purposes with one another. Specifically, some conservation programs, such as CRP, provide incentives for conversions of cropland to grassland, while farm program payments may have the unintended consequence of providing incentives for conversions of grassland to cropland. Such apparent inconsistency undermines USDA's conservation goals and the most effective use of funds. While we have identified possible cases where USDA's farm program payments work at cross purposes with its conservation programs, there could be others. Any such inconsistencies should be identified and examined in order to better inform the Congress of opportunities to improve the effectiveness and efficiency of these programs.

Appendix I

OBJECTIVES, SCOPE, AND METHODOLOGY

At the request of the Chairman, Senate Committee on Agriculture, Nutrition, and Forestry, and the Chairman, House Committee on Agriculture, we reviewed issues related to grassland conversions. Specifically, we determined (1) the extent of grassland conversions to cropland and the cost of farm program payments related to these newly converted cropland acres, (2) the relative importance of farm program payments versus other factors in producers' decisions to convert grassland to cropland, and (3) any impact the Sodbuster provision has had on limiting grassland conversions.

To determine the extent of grassland conversions to cropland, we examined land use data for 1982 through 2003 from the Natural Resources Conservation Service's (NRCS) National Resources Inventory (NRI).[1] We supplemented this information with land use data gathered by the U.S. Department of Agriculture's (USDA) National Agricultural Statistics Service (NASS).[2] In addition, we analyzed data gathered by USDA's Farm Service Agency (FSA) state and county offices in Montana, North Dakota, and South Dakota on acres converted from grassland with no cropping history to cropland for 2005 and 2006. We also reviewed a collaborative study on conversions of native grassland to cropland in the Prairie Pothole Region prepared by Ducks Unlimited, Inc., a private advocacy group supporting the protection and restoration of wetlands and waterfowl habitat, in conjunction with the U.S. Fish and Wildlife Service (FWS); the South Dakota Department of Game, Fish and Parks; The Nature Conservancy; and the University of Montana.[3] In addition, we reviewed other relevant studies of grassland conversions to cropland, including a 2001 study[4] by Texas A and M University and other researchers and a 1999 study by

University of Wisconsin researchers.[5] We interviewed USDA officials from the Economic Research Service (ERS), FSA, NASS, NRCS, and the Risk Management Agency (RMA). We also interviewed FWS state officials in Colorado, Montana, Nebraska, North Dakota, South Dakota, and Texas; state government officials; and officials at land grant universities, including Iowa State University, Kansas State University, North Dakota State University, South Dakota State University, and Texas A and M University. To determine the cost of farm program payments on converted land, we interviewed ERS and FSA officials and analyzed RMA crop insurance and FSA disaster assistance payments data. Specifically, we analyzed crop insurance and crop disaster assistance payments data in relation to 2005 and 2006 data on conversions of grassland that had no prior cropping history to cropland for all South Dakota counties. We selected South Dakota counties because conversion data were available by county for 2005 and 2006, and conversions have received considerable attention in the state. In conducting our analysis, we assumed that the counties with the most acres converted during those years were indicative of the counties with the most conversions during 1997 through 2006.

To determine the relative importance of the availability of farm program payments in producers' decisions to convert grassland to cropland, we identified and reviewed studies that directly examined the economic incentives of farm program payments on a producer's decision to convert grasslands to cropland, as well as related studies that examine the effects of farm program payments on farm profitability and risk. To evaluate how factors such as conversion costs, expected crop prices, crop production costs and technology, and farm program payments affect conversion decisions, we analyzed farm-level budget data for a hypothetical 160 acres in a South Dakota county that had a relatively high conversion rate during 2005 and 2006. The methodology for conducting this analysis was reviewed by ERS, NRCS, and land grant university agricultural economists and is discussed in appendix IV. In addition, we interviewed FSA and NRCS officials in Montana, Nebraska, North Dakota, and South Dakota to obtain their views of the importance of farm program payments and other factors in producers' decisions to convert native grassland to cropland.

To determine the impact the Sodbuster provision has had on grassland conversions, we examined NRI land use data for 1982 through 1997 and 1997 through 2003 showing conversions of rangeland to highly erodible and non-highly erodible cropland by USDA crop production regions. We supplemented these data by analyzing available NRCS data on whether land that producers intended to convert was highly erodible for selected Nebraska counties.[6] We selected these counties because the Nebraska NRCS state office had identified them as being in areas that recently had relatively high conversion rates. In addition, we conducted interviews with FSA and NRCS officials in Montana, Nebraska, North Dakota, and South Dakota to obtain their views of the impact of Sodbuster on producers' conversion decisions. We compared information obtained in these interviews with comments on Sodbuster's effectiveness submitted by NRCS field office officials in response to GAO's nationwide 2002 survey on conservation compliance issues.[7] We also interviewed FWS officials in Colorado, Montana, Nebraska, North Dakota, South Dakota, and Texas, as well as officials from industry stakeholder organizations, including the South Dakota Corn Growers Association, South Dakota Soybean Association, South Dakota Cattlemen's Association, and Montana Grain Growers Association, to obtain their views on Sodbuster's effectiveness and proposed legislative changes to reduce conversions. Finally, to identify proposed legislation that could affect payments that producers receive on newly converted land, we reviewed USDA's 2007 farm bill proposals and position papers submitted by environmental, conservation, and commodity groups, including Ducks Unlimited, Pheasants Forever, the North Dakota and South Dakota Chapters of The Wildlife Society, the North Dakota Game and Fish Department, the American Farm Bureau Federation, the National Corn Growers Association, the National Pork Producers Council, and the National Association of Wheat Growers.

We performed our work between October 2006 and August 2007 in accordance with generally accepted government auditing standards. We performed data reliability assessments for (1) FSA state office data on conversions of grassland that had no prior cropping history to cropland in Montana, North Dakota, and South Dakota, (2) crop insurance data from RMA's Summary of Business database, and (3) FSA disaster assistance payments data. We determined that data from each of these sources were sufficiently reliable. For the data obtained from the other sources noted above, we did not independently verify the data, but we discussed with these sources, as appropriate, the measures they take to ensure the accuracy of these data. For the purposes for which the data were used in this report, these measures seemed reasonable.

Appendix II

National Resources Inventory Data on Net Changes in U.S. Land Use, 1982-2003

The U.S. Department of Agriculture's Natural Resource Conservation Service's National Resources Inventory is a statistical survey of natural resource conditions and trends on nonfederal land in the United States. Nonfederal lands include privately owned lands, tribal and trust lands, and lands controlled by state and local governments. The NRI provides data on net changes in rangeland, pastureland, and other land types over time, as well as on conversions of rangeland and pastureland to cropland over time.[1] Table 7 shows the net changes in cropland, Conservation Reserve Program (CRP) land, rangeland, pastureland, and developed land, from 1982 to 2003 for the 48 contiguous states. The changes illustrated in the table are net changes, which do not indicate the number of acres converted from rangeland and pastureland to cropland.

Table 7. Net Changes in Rangeland, Pastureland, and Other Land Types, 1982-2003 acres in millions with margins of error

Year	Cropland	CRP land	Rangeland	Pastureland	Developed land
1982	419.9	0	415.5	131.1	72.9
	(417.8-422.0)	(NA)	(412.0-419.0)	(129.7-132.5)	(72.1-73.7)
1992	381.3	34.0	406.8	125.2	86.5
	(379.3-383.3)	(33.8-34.2)	(403.5-410.1)	(123.9-126.5)	(85.5-87.5)
1997	376.4	32.7	404.9	119.5	97.6
	(374.4-378.4)	(32.7-32.7)	(401.6-408.2)	(118.3-120.7)	(96.6-98.6)
2003	367.9	31.5	405.1	117.0	108.1
	(365.5-370.3)	(31.2-31.8)	(401.6-408.6)	(115.2-118.8)	(106.7-109.5)
Change,1982-2003	-52	31.5	-10.4	-14.1	35.2

Source: GAO's analysis of NRCS's NRI data.

Notes: (1) The amounts in parentheses represent the two-sided 95 percent confidence interval. (2) This table does not include other land-use categories, which did not have large changes during this period. These land-use categories are forest land, water areas, and other rural areas.

Appendix III

CENSUS OF AGRICULTURE DATA ON NET CHANGES IN USES OF LAND IN FARMS FOR THE UNITED STATES AND SELECTED STATES

The Census of Agriculture, conducted every 5 years by USDA's National Agricultural Statistics Service, is a census of agricultural producers.[1] It gathers information about the nation's agricultural production and provides agricultural data for every state and county in the United States.

Tables 8 and 9 show net changes in uses of land in farms between the years 1978 and 1992, and 1997 and 2002, as reported by the Census of Agriculture. Table 8 shows net changes in land use at the national level, while table 9 shows changes in land use for states that—according to USDA's National Resources Inventory—have large amounts of rangeland and cropland. Data for 1978 to 1992 are not comparable to data for 1997 to 2002 and are listed separately in the tables. This is because a different methodology was used for the latter time frame to more completely capture all relevant producers.

In tables 8 and 9, "Total cropland" includes cropland harvested, cropland used only for pasture or grazing, idle cropland,[2] cropland on which all crops failed or were abandoned, and cropland cultivated in summer fallow. "Pastureland and rangeland" includes all grazable land that does not qualify as cropland pasture or woodland pasture. Pastureland and rangeland includes both native grassland and grassland composed of introduced grasses. Finally, "Total land in farms" consists primarily of agricultural land used for crops, pasture, or grazing.

Table 8. Net Changes in Uses of Land in U.S. Farms, 1978-1992 and 1997-2002 acres in millions

Year	Total cropland	Pastureland and rangeland[a]	Total land in farms
1978	453.6	431.0	1011.5
1982	445.1	416.0	983.5
1987	442.9	408.4	961.8
1992	435.0	409.1	943.0
Change in acres,1978-1992	-18.6	-21.9	-68.5
1997	444.9	396.6	952.5
2002	433.9	393.7	936.1
Change in acres, 1997-2002	-11.0	-2.9	-16.5

Source: GAO's analysis of NASS's Census of Agriculture data.

[a] The full name of this category is Pastureland and rangeland, other than cropland and woodland pastured.

Table 9. Net Changes in Uses of Land in Farms in States with Large Amounts of Rangeland and Pastureland, 1978-1992 and.1997-2002

acres in millions				
State	Year	Total cropland	Pastureland and rangeland	Total land in farms
Colorado	1978	10.6	22.7	35.3
	1992	10.9	21.3	34.0
	Change in acres, 1978-1992	0.3	-1.4	-1.3
	1997	10.8	19.4	32.3
	2002	11.5	17.3	31.1
	Change in acres, 1997-2002	0.7	-2.1	-1.3
Kansas	1978	29.8	15.5	47.5
	1992	31.1	13.8	46.7
	Change in acres, 1978-1992	1.3	-1.8	-0.8
	1997	31.1	13.6	46.7
	2002	29.5	15.5	47.2
	Change in acres, 1997-2002	-1.5	1.9	0.6

acres in millions				
State	Year	Total cropland	Pastureland and rangeland	Total land in farms
Montana	1978	16.2	42.4	61.7
	1992	17.5	39.3	59.6
	Change in acres, 1978-1992	1.3	-3.1	-2.0
	1997	18.2	37.2	58.4
	2002	18.3	38.2	59.6
	Change in acres, 1997-2002	0.8	1.1	1.2
Nebraska	1978	22.3	22.1	46.1
	1992	22.4	20.6	44.4
	Change in acres, 1978-1992	0.1	-1.6	-1.7
	1997	22.6	21.6	45.9
	2002	22.5	21.9	45.9
	Change in acres, 1997-2002	-0.1	0.3	0.05
New Mexico	1978	2.3	42.5	47.9
	1992	2.3	42.0	46.8
	Change in acres, 1978-1992	-0.004	-0.5	-1.1
	1997	2.3	41.0	46.2
	2002	2.6	39.1	44.8
	Change in acres, 1997-2002	0.3	-1.8	-1.4
North Dakota	1978	28.6	10.8	41.7
	1992	27.5	10.3	39.4
	Change in acres, 1978-1992	-1.1	-0.5	-2.3
	1997	27.4	10.3	39.7
	2002	26.5	11.0	39.3
	Change in acres, 1997-2002	-0.9	0.7	-0.4
Oklahoma	1978	14.4	16.5	33.7
	1992	14.5	15.1	32.1
	Change in acres, 1978-1992	0.2	-1.5	-1.6
	1997	15.5	15.5	34.1
	2002	14.8	15.7	33.7
	Change in acres, 1997-2002	-0.6	0.2	-0.4

Table 9. (Continued).

acres in millions				
State	Year	Total cropland	Pastureland and rangeland	Total land in farms
South Dakota	1978	18.7	24.2	44.4
	1992	19.6	23.9	44.8
	Change in acres, 1978-1992	0.8	-0.2	0.4
	1997	19.7	23.0	44.1
	2002	20.3	22.0	43.8
	Change in acres, 1997-2002	0.6	-1.0	-0.4
Texas	1978	39.4	87.3	135.6
	1992	36.4	87.8	130.9
	Change in acres, 1978-1992	-3.0	0.5	-4.7
	1997	39.1	86.9	134.0
	2002	38.7	83.4	129.9
	Change in acres, 1997-2002	-0.4	-3.5	-4.1
Wyoming	1978	2.7	30.1	33.6
	1992	2.8	28.9	32.9
	Change in acres, 1978-1992	0.1	-1.2	-0.8
	1997	3.0	30.2	34.3
	2002	3.0	30.2	34.4
	Change in acres, 1997-2002	0.0	0.1	0.1

Source: GAO's analysis of NASS's Census of Agriculture data.

Appendix IV

Partial Budget Analysis for a Proposed Conversion of Native Grassland to Cropland in Central South Dakota, 2003-2007

To assess the economic incentives to convert native grassland to cropland at the farm level, we used a partial budget analysis and a "constructed" farm scenario for a 160-acre tract in Hand County, South Dakota—a central South Dakota county that was relatively high in 2005 and 2006 conversions of grassland that had no cropping history. A partial budget can be used by a farmer or rancher to evaluate the economic effects of making an adjustment to a part of the farm operation, such as switching to an alternative farm enterprise or buying new machinery. While not including all farm costs and revenues of the enterprise, a partial budget[1] estimates the net change in income that results when shifting from a base plan to an alternative scenario.[2]

Livestock grazing enterprises, in particular cow-calf operations, have historically been typical farm enterprises in South Dakota. In recent years, however, some of the land that was used for grazing has been converted to crop production. To analyze the role of farm program payments in these conversions, we developed a partial budget to compare the estimated costs and returns for 2003 through 2007 from 160 acres of native grassland—used for grazing as part of a cow-calf operation—to the costs and returns that would have resulted if the 160 acres had been converted to cropland in 2003 and used to produce corn, soybeans, and wheat through 2007. We assumed that the farm operation initially consisted of both a cropping enterprise and a

cow-calf enterprise. Therefore, the farmer already had certain fixed capital equipment for both of these enterprises, such as tractors and harvesting equipment. In the base plan, the producer had a 160-acre parcel of native grassland that was part of a larger cow-calf grazing enterprise.

We analyzed cow-calf and crop budgets (1) prospectively for the current 2007 crop year and (2) retrospectively for crop years 2003 through 2006 to specifically evaluate the effects of past farm program payments on costs and returns. During these years, crop and calf prices varied and central South Dakota experienced a range of weather conditions that affected crop and forage production. These changes in price and production make these years illustrative for analysis of the effect farm program payments can have on farm enterprises.

We found that for certain years, high crop prices as well as farm program payments would provide economic incentives for a producer to convert native grassland used for grazing in a cow-calf operation to an alternative cropping operation. In 3 of the 5 years, the conversion from grazing to cropping would have resulted in increased income. In the other 2 years, 2004 and 2005, when cattle prices and returns were high relative to crop prices and returns and total farm program payments were lower, it would have been more profitable not to convert and continue the cow-calf operation. Without any farm program payments, income would have increased only in 2007, but in view of projections that crop prices will remain relatively high, this increase in income without farm program payments may continue for several years. However, even with high crop prices, farm program payments for crop insurance and crop disaster assistance will continue to be an important factor in conversion decisions because of the need for protection against adverse crop production risks, such as drought.

BASE PLAN SCENARIO—COW-CALF GRAZING

For the base plan or cow-calf section of the analysis, we used production and price data from South Dakota State University's cow-calf budget tool[3] as well as expert opinion from South Dakota State University livestock extension economists and USDA Natural Resources Conservation Service officials in South Dakota. We assumed that Hand County, South Dakota, in a normal year of precipitation, would support one cow-calf pair for every 8 acres of native grassland. Since South Dakota experienced varied weather conditions—including drought—during 2003 through 2007, we adjusted our

cow-calf model to incorporate changes in the number of pounds of calves and cows sold to account for changes in the amount of forage available for grazing on the 160 acres. These adjustments were based on NRCS rangeland forage production values for favorable, normal, and unfavorable years.[4] On the basis of South Dakota NRCS officials' expert opinion, we assumed that a 20 percent deviation in annual rainfall above or below the 30-year average during 1976 through 2006 would be either favorable or unfavorable, respectively. Using this definition, 2003 forage production values were normal, 2004 were favorable, 2005 were normal, and 2006 were unfavorable. We assumed 2007 forage production values were normal based on South Dakota NRCS officials' observations as of July 2007.

In estimating cow-calf returns, we used calf prices from South Dakota State University's stocker cattle prices (500 to 600 pounds), monthly average prices, for November. For cull cow prices, we used the Sioux Falls price of slaughter cows for November 2003 through 2006; for 2007, we used an average of the first 5 months of the year. For additional income due to herd liquidation, we obtained yearly average "Bred Female" prices, Central Region, for "young and middle-aged cows" from Drovers for 2003 through 2006 and the first 5 months of 2007.[5] For corn feed costs, we calculated an average price for each year, 2003 through 2006, based on weekly Central South Dakota cash corn prices from South Dakota State University's extension service; for 2007, we calculated an average of these weekly prices from January to July. For hay alfalfa prices, we used USDA National Agricultural Statistics Service yearly average prices for 2003 through 2006, and for 2007, an average monthly price based on the first 5 months of this year. Regarding "other" costs, we reduced all direct costs in the cow-calf spreadsheet before 2005 by 10 percent, with the exception of "Veterinary and Drug," which we reduced by 15 percent, and kept all the later years the same as in the budget tool spreadsheet.[6]

Alternative Scenario—Corn/Soybean/Spring Wheat Cropping Rotation

For the alternative scenario—the crop portion of the partial budget analysis, we assumed a corn/soybean/spring wheat crop rotation on the 160-acre parcel for a farm in Hand County, South Dakota. We assumed this particular crop rotation based on those crops having the highest acreages according to NASS statistics and consultations with South Dakota State

University crop extension experts. We first looked retrospectively at the time period from 2003 through 2006 to see the effects of prices, yields, and farm payments on costs and returns. We then used preliminary data for crop prices and average historical yield data to examine potential returns for crop year 2007.[7]

For 2003 through 2007, we adjusted all yield data to reflect the fact that this newly converted land may represent "marginal" or less productive land than the land that was already in crop production. To do this, we consulted with NRCS officials in central South Dakota to obtain information on the soil types that were most often being converted.[8] On the basis of this information, we then adjusted the county average crop yields for corn, soybeans, and spring wheat to estimate a likely yield for a newly converted parcel of native grassland for a particular year. On average, these estimated yields were about 17 percent lower than the county average yields. We used these adjusted yields in our calculation of gross income from corn, soybeans, and spring wheat in our partial budget analysis. In addition, because documentation on the soil types most often being converted was not available and to determine how sensitive our results were to these adjusted crop yields, we also estimated gross returns from crop production in our partial budget analysis using unadjusted NASS county average crop yields for 2003 through 2006. For 2007, we estimated an unadjusted 3-year moving county average for corn and soybeans, and for spring wheat, we used the South Dakota NASS yield projection as of July 2007.

We obtained the remaining data on prices and costs for the crop analysis from extension specialists and agricultural economists in central South Dakota and at South Dakota State University.[9] For instance, we obtained most of the cost data for the crop budgets from an area farm management specialist in the Department of Economics at South Dakota State University. For price data, we used yearly average central South Dakota cash prices for corn, soybeans, and spring wheat for 2003 through 2006 from South Dakota State University's extension grain marketing specialist. For 2007 price data, we used the most recent statewide average cash price, as of July 13, for South Dakota for corn, soybeans, and spring wheat. For 2003 through 2006 loan deficiency payments, we used Hand County average yearly loan deficiency payments for this period from the USDA Farm Service Agency's South Dakota state office.[10] For crop insurance payments to farmers, we used crop insurance indemnity payments per acre in Hand County, South Dakota as estimated by a USDA Risk Management Agency official. For crop disaster assistance payments, we used data from FSA on crop disaster assistance payments by county to estimate an average crop disaster assistance payment per acre for Hand County for 2003, the only year when these payments were significant.[11] Because crop insurance indemnity and crop disaster assistance payments generally are related to the same crop losses, we used RMA crop insurance indemnity payments data in making this estimate. Specifically, we applied the proportion of the amount of crop insurance indemnities that were paid to each crop (i.e., corn, soybeans, and spring wheat) to the total crop disaster assistance payments in the county for 2003 to estimate the crop disaster assistance payment for each crop.

In addition to income from crop production, the producer's additional returns in the first year of conversion would be from the sale or liquidation of the herd that had grazed on the 160-acre parcel. Specifically, we assumed the conversion takes place in 2003, and the herd liquidation in a normal year would consist of about 20 bred females that previously grazed on the land, of which 10 would be sold in the bred female market and 10 in the cull cow market since the cow herd would be composed of various ages. In order not to disproportionately influence any one year's returns from the herd liquidation, the proceeds were amortized over a 5-year period, from 2003 to 2007, at an interest rate of 6 percent, resulting in annual revenue of about \$3,125. Similarly, as part of the conversion, we also assumed conversion costs for the 160-acre parcel of land, consisting of about \$3,200 for herbicide treatment, would be amortized over this period, resulting in an annual cost of about \$760. According to NRCS officials, rock removal can also add to conversion costs, but these costs are highly variable because the amount of rocks on native grass and the methods used in removing them varies. Thus, we did not include rock removal in our partial budget analysis.

As noted, we assumed the conversion to cropland occurred in 2003. The use of another year for the conversion would have some effect on the results. For example, if the conversion had occurred in 2004, a year of relatively high cattle prices and better forage available for grazing, the revenue from the cow liquidation would have been greater. In that year, the amortized annual value from the sale of the cow herd would have been \$4,284, about \$1,158 greater than in 2003. Thus, the annual net change in income resulting from the conversion to cropland would have been about \$1,158 higher.

Partial Budget Analysis

After creating the base plan and alternative scenario and collecting the appropriate data for the 5 years, we then used these data in the partial budget to analyze the role of farm program payments in conversion decisions and determine which option, the cow-calf enterprise or the cropping enterprise, would provide higher returns over costs. Specifically, as table 10 shows, the alternative scenario—conversion to cropland—would result in additional returns from crop production, farm program payments, and the sale of the cow herd (Section 1), reduced costs from no longer having the present cow-calf enterprise (Section 2), additional costs from crop production (including conversion costs) (Section 3), and reduced returns from the cow-calf enterprise (Section 4). Therefore, in the partial budget analysis, the net change in income for the producer would be the total benefits of the proposed change (Sections 1 and 2) minus the total costs (Sections 3 and 4).

The partial budget results for crop years 2003 through 2006 are shown in table 10. For each year, we estimated the net change in income using crop yields adjusted for soil productivity. As noted earlier, we also estimated these income changes using unadjusted NASS county average crop yields. In 2003, the sum of gross revenue from the sale of crops produced, farm program payments (crop insurance, crop disaster assistance, and loan deficiency payments), and the amortized proceeds from the liquidation of the cow herd would have resulted in a positive change in net income of $3,761 in favor of the alternative scenario, crop production using the adjusted crop yields. Although 2003 cash corn prices were at relatively average historical levels, $2.36 per bushel, and soybean prices were high, averaging about $7.70 per bushel, yields were at very low levels resulting in relatively low crop revenue. However, farm program payments would have offset this low crop revenue, contributing approximately $12,300 on the 160-acre tract. Without these farm program payments, net income from the base plan, the cow-calf enterprise, would have been about $8,500 greater than crop production in this year. Using the unadjusted county average, crop yields would have produced a net change in income of about $6,824 in favor of the cropping alternative.

For 2004, we estimate net income of about $3,602 in favor of remaining with the base plan, the cow-calf enterprise. Although crop yields were relatively high in 2004, corn and soybean prices were much lower than the previous year, at $1.64 and $5.49, respectively. Also, the total of crop insurance, crop disaster assistance, and loan deficiency payments for this year were almost $9,000 lower than in 2003. Although loan deficiency payments were higher due to the lower crop prices, crop insurance benefits were lower due to the higher crop yields, and crop disaster assistance payments would not have been made because, as provided in the legislation, the producer could only receive a crop disaster assistance payment for 2003 or 2004 and could not receive a payment for both years. Moreover, 2004 cow-calf returns were relatively high, as calf prices had increased over 2003, going from an average of $111 to $122 per hundredweight. In addition, we estimate higher returns to the cow-calf enterprise in this year due to more favorable weather for forage production and lower prices for feedstuffs. Furthermore, direct costs of production for the cow-calf enterprise (about $6,500) were about one-third that of the costs of production for the cropping enterprise (about $19,500). However, using unadjusted county average yields to estimate gross revenue causes the alternative scenario, conversion to cropland, to be higher in net income, but only by about $1,375.

Similarly, for 2005, we estimate that net income from the alternative scenario, crop production, with yields adjusted for soil productivity would have been about $4,835 less than the base plan, the cow-calf enterprise. The net change in income using the unadjusted county average crop yields would have been higher for the alternative scenario by about $90. In 2005, crop yields were similar to those in 2004, but crop prices were again quite low. At the same time, calf prices were at historically high levels—$137 per hundredweight. Feedstuff costs, due to the low corn prices, were relatively low, and the costs of production for cropping were over three times greater than costs for the cow-calf enterprise. Also, in 2005, while some loan deficiency payments ($2,175 for the 160-acre parcel) were received, crop insurance payments, about $625 for the parcel, were much lower than the previous year, and no crop disaster assistance payments had been received as of July 2007.

For 2006, we estimate an increase net income of about $2,366 in favor of the alternative scenario, crop production. Although crop yields were very low due to drought, crop prices increased. Average cash corn prices for Central South Dakota jumped from $1.76 per bushel in 2005 to $3.37 per bushel in 2006. More importantly, however, due to the low yields that year, the producer would have received about $8,995 on the 160-acre parcel from crop insurance payments.[12] At the same time, cow-calf returns decreased because of decreases in calf and cow prices and unfavorable conditions for forage production because of the drought. This reduced forage production would result in lower calf weights and higher feed costs for the cow-calf enterprise. Using the unadjusted NASS county average crop yields would have increased the net income change to about $6,069.

Table 10. Partial Budget Analysis for a Proposed 2003 Change from a Cow-Calf Enterprise to a Corn/Soybean/Wheat Cropping Enterprise in Central South Dakota, 2003-2006

Partial budget, 2003	Amount of change	
	Adjusted crop yields	County average crop yields
Section 1		
Additional returns from proposed change		
Corn	$4,666.73	$5,610.14
Soybeans	4,063.06	4,883.88
Spring wheat	6,120.97	7,349.00
Loan deficiency payment	351.14	421.71
Crop insurance payment	7,895.33	7,895.33
Disaster assistance payment	4,014.02	4,014.02
Liquidation of cow herd (amortized)	3,125.23	3,125.23
Subtotal additional returns	$30,236.49	$33,299.32
Section 2		
Reduced costs from proposed change		
Reduced costs from cow-calf operation	$5,473.62	$5,473.62
Subtotal reduced costs	$5,473.62	$5,473.62
Section 3		
Additional costs of proposed change		
Corn	$7,330.88	$7,330.88
Soybeans	4,770.35	4,770.35
Spring wheat	5,039.52	5,039.52
Herbicide treatment for	759.67	759.67
conversion (amortized)		
Subtotal additional costs	$17,900.42	$17,900.42
Section 4		
Reduced returns from proposed change		
Sale of calves and cull cows in a year with normal forage production	$14,048.49	$14,048.49
Subtotal reduced returns	$14,048.49	$14,048.49
Net change in income, 2003	$3,761.20	$6,824.03
Partial budget, 2004	Amount of change	
	Adjusted crop yields	County average crop yields
Section 1		
Additional returns from proposed change		
Corn	$7,377.57	$8,863.58
Soybeans	7,373.95	8,866.30
Spring wheat	8,029.96	9,662.22
Loan deficiency payment	1,817.32	2,184.39
Crop insurance payment	1,211.51	1,211.51
Disaster assistance payment	—	—

Partial budget, 2003	Amount of change	
	Adjusted crop yields	County average crop yields
Liquidation of cow herd (amortized)	3,125.23	3,125.23
Subtotal additional returns	$28,935.54	$33,913.23
Section 2		
Reduced costs from proposed change		
Reduced costs from cow-calf operation	$6,570.14	$6,570.14
Subtotal reduced costs	$6,570.14	$6,570.14
Section 3		
Additional costs of proposed change		
Corn	$8,568.51	$8,568.51
Soybeans	4,796.47	4,796.47
Spring wheat	6,163.61	6,163.61
Herbicide treatment for conversion (amortized)	759.67	759.67
Subtotal additional costs	$20,288.26	$20,288.26
Section 4		
Reduced returns from proposed change		
Sale of calves and cull cows in a year with favorable forage production	$18,820.18	$18,820.18
Subtotal reduced returns	$18,820.18	$18,820.18
Net change in income, 2004	($3,602.75)	$1,374.94
Partial budget, 2005	Amount of change	
	Adjusted crop yields	County average crop yields
Section 1		
Additional returns from proposed change		
Corn	$7,617.21	$9,155.66
Soybeans	7,416.70	8,927.00
Spring wheat	7,079.57	8,516.01
Loan deficiency payment	2,174.75	2,614.15
Crop insurance payment	625.21	625.21
Disaster assistance payment	—	—
Liquidation of cow herd (amortized)	3,125.23	3,125.23
Subtotal additional returns	$28,038.66	$32,963.26
Section 2		
Reduced costs from proposed change		
Reduced costs from cow-calf operation	$5,737.80	$5,737.80
Subtotal reduced costs	$5,737.80	$5,737.80
Section 3		
Additional costs of proposed change		
Corn	$9,187.85	$9,187.85
Soybeans	5,344.39	5,344.39
Spring wheat	6,459.43	6,459.43

Table 10. (Continued).

Partial budget, 2003	Amount of change	
	Adjusted crop yields	County average crop yields
Herbicide treatment for conversion (amortized)	759.67	759.67
Subtotal additional costs	$21,751.34	$21,751.34
Section 4		
Reduced returns from proposed change		
Sale of calves and cull cows in a year with normal forage production	$16,859.78	$16,859.78
Subtotal reduced returns	$16,859.78	$16,859.78
Net change in income, 2005	($4,834.66)	$89.94
Partial budget, 2006		
	Amount of change	
	Adjusted crop yields	County average crop yields
Section 1		
Additional returns from proposed change		
Corn	$7,454.27	$8,963.09
Soybeans	5,632.64	6,752.58
Spring wheat	5,197.82	6,252.09
Loan deficiency payment	100.26	120.19
Crop insurance payment	8,995.44	8,995.44
Disaster assistance payment	—	—
Liquidation of cow herd (amortized)	$3,125.23	$3,125.23
Subtotal additional returns	$30,505.65	$34,208.62
Section 2		
Reduced costs from proposed change		
Reduced costs from cow-calf operation	$4,609.36	$4,609.36
Subtotal reduced costs	$4,609.36	$4,609.36
Section 3		
Additional costs of proposed change		
Corn	$9,707.00	$9,707.00
Soybeans	5,617.82	5,617.82
Spring wheat	7,043.06	7,043.06
Herbicide treatment for conversion (amortized)	759.67	759.67
Subtotal additional costs	$23,127.55	$23,127.55
Section 4		
Reduced returns from proposed change		
Sale of calves and cull cows in a year with unfavorable forage production	$9,621.12	$9,621.12
Subtotal reduced returns	$9,621.12	$9,621.12
Net change in income, 2006	$2,366.35	$6,069.31

Source: GAO's analysis based on data provided by and consultations with South Dakota State University, FSA, NASS, NRCS, and RMA. Partial budget template used by permission of the Agricultural Economics Department, University of Missouri.

Notes: (1) We calculated returns and costs assuming conversion of native grassland to cropland on a "constructed" farm in Hand County, South Dakota that produced a rotation of corn, soybeans, and spring wheat. (2) For the crop enterprise, we used regional average crop prices; NASS county average crop yields, both adjusted and unadjusted for soil productivity; central South Dakota region crop production cost data; and county average crop insurance, and crop disaster assistance, and loan deficiency payments. We used assumptions and data provided by agricultural economists, agronomists, and soil scientists from South Dakota State University and NASS to estimate yields and conversion costs. Farm program payments data were provided by FSA and RMA officials. (3) Data and assumptions for the cow-calf enterprise are from South Dakota State University extension service in the central and eastern regions and NRCS officials in South Dakota. We did not include in our analysis the benefits from any livestock disaster assistance payments, although we realize there were such payments in 2004. For feed prices, we used average weekly cash corn prices for the Central region of South Dakota, from the South Dakota State University extension service and yearly NASS prices for alfalfa hay. (4) The dashes indicate that we did not include a crop disaster assistance payment for 2004, 2005, or 2006.

We also estimated the income effects of converting native grassland to crop production prospectively for the current 2007 crop year. As table 11 shows for 2007, we estimate that the net change in income for the alternative scenario, crop production, would be about $2,099. Also, in this high price year for crops, the value of production from the cropping enterprise would be about $15,000 more than from the cow-calf enterprise. An important factor for the cow-calf enterprise during this year would be the adjustment to much higher feed prices, which along with lower calf prices, would lead to lower cow-calf returns in 2007. On the crop side, because 2007 crop prices are forecast to stay above the marketing loan rates, we assumed no loan deficiency payments would be received for this year. In addition, we did not include any crop insurance or disaster assistance payments for 2007, although such payments may be made in the future. Despite the absence of farm program payments, the partial budget demonstrates that in this high crop price year crop production would have been more profitable than using the land for grazing cattle. Using the unadjusted 2007 projected county average yields would increase the net income resulting from the conversion to cropland to about $8,290.

Table 11. Partial Budget Analysis for a Proposed 2003 Change from a Cow-Calf Enterprise to a Corn/Soybean/Wheat Cropping Enterprise in Central South Dakota, 2007

Partial budget, 2007		
	Amount of change	
	Adjusted crop yields	Projected and average crop yields
Section 1		
Additional returns from proposed change		
Corn	$12,951.13	$15,566.50
Soybeans	8,335.76	10,018.18
Spring wheat	9,382.80	11,276.15
Loan deficiency payment	—	—
Crop insurance payment	—	—
Disaster assistance payment	—	—
Liquidation of cow herd	3,125.23	3,125.23
(amortized)		
Subtotal additional returns	$33,794.92	$39,986.06
Section 2		
Reduced costs from proposed change		
Reduced costs from cow-calf operation	$7,187.80	$7,187.80
Subtotal reduced costs	$7,187.80	$7,187.80
Section 3		
Additional costs of proposed change		
Corn	$9,726.18	$9,726.18
Soybeans	5,573.05	5,573.05
Spring wheat	7,324.49	7,324.49
Herbicide treatment for	759.67	759.67
conversion (amortized)		
Subtotal additional costs	$23,383.39	$23,383.39
Section 4		
Reduced returns from proposed change		
Sale of calves and cull cows in a year with unfavorable forage production	$15,499.86	$15,499.86
Subtotal reduced returns	$15,499.86	$15,499.86
Net change in income, 2007	$2,099.47	$8,290.61

Source: GAO's analysis based on data provided by and consultations with South Dakota State University extension service, NASS, and NRCS. Partial budget template used by permission of the Agricultural Economics Department, University of Missouri.

Notes: (1) We calculated returns and costs assuming conversion of native grassland to cropland on a "constructed" farm in Hand County, South Dakota, that produced a rotation of corn, soybeans, and spring wheat. (2) For the crop enterprise, we used regional average crop prices for January to July 2007; a 3-year moving average of NASS county average crop yields, adjusted and unadjusted for soil productivity for corn and soybeans and a projected 2007 South Dakota yield for spring wheat, adjusted and unadjusted for soil productivity; and central South Dakota regional crop production cost data. We used assumptions and data provided by NRCS officials to estimate conversion costs. (3) Data and assumptions for the cow-calf enterprise are from South Dakota State University extension service in the central and eastern regions and NRCS officials in South Dakota. For 2007, we used 2007 average weekly cash corn prices for the central region of South Dakota from January to July from the South Dakota State University extension service and January to June average monthly NASS prices for alfalfa hay. (4) The dashes indicate that no loan deficiency payments would be received for 2007 and that we did not include any crop insurance or disaster assistance payments for this year, although such payments may be made in the future.

In summary, if South Dakota corn, soybean, and wheat prices stay at relatively high levels, as forecast by USDA national price projections, incentives for conversion should continue in the near future.[13] In addition, as the retrospective analysis suggests, farm program payments, especially crop insurance and crop disaster assistance payments, lower the risk of negative returns in years with low crop yields.

Appendix V

SUMMARIES OF ECONOMIC STUDIES EXAMINING THE IMPACT OF FARM PROGRAM PAYMENTS

We identified and reviewed 15 studies that analyze the potential economic impacts of federal farm program payments on either producers' land use decisions or farm profitability and risk. The impact of farm program payments on farm profitability and risk is closely related to land use decisions. Table 12 summarizes the 15 studies, including the purpose and results associated with each.

Table 12. Economic Studies That Analyze the Impact of Federal Farm Program Payments on Either Producers' Land Use Decisions or Farm Profitability and Risk

Economic study	Purpose of the study	Year	Related findings and conclusions
Janssen, Larry, Burton Pflueger, and Terry Ahrendt. *South Dakota Agricultural Land Market Trends, 1991-2007*. South Dakota State University Agricultural Experiment Station, USDA.	To report on current agricultural land values and cash rental rates by land use in different regions in South Dakota.	2007	Land values in South Dakota have doubled since 2002 and tripled since 1996. During this time, farm commodity payments increased from $230 million to more than $700 million a year. In addition to commodity payments, interest rates, technology, and ethanol demand have also been factors in increasing land values. However, farmland values have become more dependent on farm program payments.
Shaik, Saleem, Joseph Atwood, and Glenn Helmbers. "Farm Programs and Agricultural Land Values: The Case of Southern Agriculture." Paper presented to the Southern Agricultural Economics Association Annual Meetings, Orlando, Florida, February 2006.	To examine the contribution of expected farm returns and farm program payments in 12 southern states.	2006	The proportion of land values attributable to farm program payments has increased from about 14 percent in the early 1980's to 67 percent in the southern United States from 2002 to 2004.

Economic study	Purpose of the study	Year	Related findings and conclusions
U.S. Department of Agriculture. Economic Research Service. *Environmental Effects of Agricultural Land-Use Change: The Role of Economics and Policy*. Economic Research Report Number 25, Washington, D.C., August 2006.	To examine the relationship between agricultural land use changes, soil productivity, and environmental sensitivity and the effects of increased crop insurance subsidies on land use.	2006	Land moving between cultivated cropland and less intensive agricultural uses is less productive and more vulnerable to erosion and nutrient runoff than other cultivated land. Producers tend to keep highly productive land in cultivation regardless of changing economic conditions. But economic conditions, such as changing commodity prices or production costs, encourage farmers to expand production to less productive land or to shift less productive croplands to other uses. Agricultural and conservation policies also affect land use. These land use changes affect environmental quality, particularly when affected lower-quality lands are environmentally sensitive. Crop insurance raises incentives to expand crops to less productive land. Increased crop insurance subsidies in the mid-1990s motivated producers to expand cropland in the contiguous 48 states by an estimated 2.5 million acres, with most of the land coming from pastureland and other grassland. Due to this land-use change, annual wind and water erosion estimates increased by 1.4 and 0.9 percent, respectively, as of 1997.

Table 12. (Continued).

Economic study	Purpose of the study	Year	Related findings and conclusions
U.S. Department of Agriculture. Economic Research Service. *Agricultural Resources and Environmental Indicators, 2006 Edition.* Economic Information Bulletin 16, Washington, D.C., July 2006.	To describe patterns and trends in land, water, and biological resources; report on the condition of natural and other resources used in the agricultural sector; and describe public policies and programs as well as economic factors that affect resource use, conservation, and environmental quality in agriculture.	2006	Previous research has shown that capitalization of expected farm program payments increases cropland values. The effect of farm program payments on cropland values varies widely throughout the United States, but increases are highest in the Northern Plains.
Janssen, Larry, and Yonas Hamda. Federal Farm Program Payments (1990 – 2001): An Analysis of Changing Dependency and the Distribution of Farm Payments in South Dakota. Selected paper 136474 presented to the American Agricultural Economics Association Annual Meetings, Providence, Rhode Island, July 2005.	To examine the economic impact of federal farm program payments in South Dakota at the state and local levels from 1996 to 2001.	2005	Statewide, federal farm program payments averaged 36 percent of net farm income from 1990 to 1995 and almost 54 percent from 1996 to 2001. The lowest dependency rate of net farm income on payments was in the most cropland-intensive East Central/Southeast region, while the highest dependency rate was in the Western region, which was the only region with payments exceeding net farm income in most years examined. The dependency rate of farm income on payments increased considerably in all regions from the 1990-1995 time period to the 1996-2001 period.

Economic study	Purpose of the study	Year	Related findings and conclusions
Economic study Babcock, Bruce, and Chad Hart. "Risk-Free Farming?" *Iowa Ag Review*, vol. 10. no. 1 (Winter 2004), 1-3,11.	Purpose of the study To examine how farm programs and crop insurance affect revenue.	Year 2004	Related findings and conclusions The reduction in risk that crop farmers obtain from crop insurance and commodity programs has largely resulted in risk-free crop production. In addition, the article states that farm programs create incentives for farmers and landlords to focus on growing the commodities that are supported by these programs.
Goodwin, Barry, Ashok Mishra, and Francois Ortolo-Magne. "Landowners' Riches: The Distribution of Agricultural Subsidies." (Madison, Wisconsin: University of Wisconsin, February 2004). www.busc.wisc.edu/Realestate/pdf/ Landownersriches.pdf (downloaded June 21, 2007).	To examine the distribution of farm program payments and how landowners may benefit from these payments.	2004	Farm program subsidies have a significant impact on farm land values. Among the types of payments studied, loan deficiency payments appear to have the largest effect. Long-term payments not directly related to production had relatively little impact.
Gray, Allan, Michael Boehlje, Brent Gloy, and Stephen Slinksy. "How U.S. Farm Programs and Crop Revenue Insurance Affect Returns to Farm Land," *Review of Agricultural Economics*, vol. 26, no. 2 (2004), pp. 238-253.	To examine the economic impact of federal farm program and crop insurance payments on a typical Northwest Indiana corn/soybean farm.	2004	Federal farm program payments influence land use decisions because they increase the expected returns to farming while lowering the associated risk. Also, crop revenue insurance enhanced the impact of other farm programs by substantially increasing the attractiveness of farming for the most risk-averse producers.

Table 12. (Continued).

Economic study	Purpose of the study	Year	Related findings and conclusions
Smith, Katherine. "The Growing Prevalence of Emergency, Disaster, and Other Ad Hoc Farm Program Payments: Implications for Agri-Environmental and Conservation Programs," *Agricultural and Resource Economics Review*, vol. 30, no.1 (2004): 1-7.	To examine various federal disaster assistance programs to determine potential reasons for the rise in ad hoc disaster payments and their impact on agri-environmental and conservation programs.	2004	The use of emergency, disaster, and other ad hoc sources of income support to American farmers escalated dramatically between 1991 and 2002, increasing year-to- year uncertainty about the magnitude and distribution of farm program benefits. Ad hoc payments have the potential to substitute for or conflict with agri-environmental and conservation program goals. Crop disaster payments mitigate risk for risk-averse producers, thus increasing risky production, which, in turn, could lead to more natural and market-based losses. This could increase the need for additional crop insurance and disaster payments.

Economic study	Purpose of the study	Year	Related findings and conclusions
Economic study Goodwin, Barry, and Vincent Smith, "An Ex Post Evaluation of the Conservation Reserve, Federal Crop Insurance, and Other Government Programs: Program Participation and Soil Erosion," *Journal of Agricultural and Resource Economics*, vol. 28, no. 2 (2003): 201-216.	Purpose of the study To examine the impact of federal farm programs on soil erosion.	Year 2003	Related findings and conclusions The Conservation Reserve Program significantly reduced soil erosion in areas where producers have participated. While federal crop insurance and disaster relief programs appear to have had little impact on soil erosion, income supports that have encouraged production have had substantial effects. In particular, about half of the reduction in soil erosion attributable to CRP enrollment was offset by increased erosion induced by increases in income-supporting federal programs.
Federal Reserve Bank of St. Louis. *Political Allocation of U.S. Agriculture Disaster Payments in the 1990s*. Working paper 2003-005C (St. Louis, Missouri, 2003).	To examine the impact of political influence on the allocation of crop disaster payments, in addition to the effectiveness of legislation aimed at promoting more efficient disaster payments systems, such as crop insurance, over direct payments.	2003	The report cites earlier studies finding that crop disaster payments create an incentive for producers to continue farming in high-risk areas, therefore continuing the likelihood of losses and the need for assistance. Also, because individual production histories are not always available, county averages are often used to determine disaster payments, and producers farming less than the county average receive payments exceeding their actual losses. Finally, disaster payments do not have predictable annual costs.

Table 12. (Continued).

Economic study	Purpose of the study	Year	Related findings and conclusions
Young, C. Edwin, Monte Vandeveer, and Randal Schnepf. "Production and Price Impacts of U.S. Crop Insurance Programs," *American Journal of Agricultural Economics*, vol. 83, no. 5 (2001), 1196-1203.	To examine the impact of federal crop insurance on farmers' crop decision making.	2001	The presence of subsidized crop insurance adds an estimated 960,000 acres to the annual planting of grain, soybean, cotton, and five other row crops for the years 2001- 2010, with more than half of these plantings occurring in the Great Plains. To the extent that subsidized crop insurance leads to expanded acreage and higher production, market returns to producers will be reduced for the major crops. This reduction partially offsets the subsidy benefits of the insurance.

Economic study	Purpose of the study	Year	Related findings and conclusions
Claassen, Roger, and Abebayehu Tegene, “Agricultural Land Use Choice: A Discrete Choice Approach,” *Agricultural and Resource Economics Review* (1999), 26-36.	To examine the impact of certain economic and land quality factors on land use choices between crop production and pasture or CRP in the Corn Belt between 1980 and 1987.	1999	Conversion probabilities depend on the relative returns from crop production and pasture, government policy (CRP), and land quality. In general it is found that landowners are less inclined to remove land from crop production than to convert land to crop production. Corn Belt landowners appear to be generally less inclined to remove land from crop production than to convert land to crop production for land that was not eligible for the CRP. This is true even for low-quality land that was not eligible for the CRP. The asymmetry found here is consistent with a long-term trend toward increasing cropland acreage in the Corn Belt. CRP eligibility significantly increased the probability of converting land away from crop production.

Table 12. (Continued).

Economic study	Purpose of the study	Year	Related findings and conclusions
Economic study Atwood, Joseph, Myles Watts, and Alan Baquet. "An Examination of the Effects of Price Supports and Federal Crop Insurance upon the Economic Growth, Capital Structure, and Financial Survival of Wheat Growers in the Northern High Plains," *American Journal of Agricultural Economics*, vol. 78, no. 1 (February 1996), 212-214.	Purpose of the study To examine the economic impact of federal farm program and crop insurance payments on wheat producers in High Plains states, such as Montana.	Year 1996	Related findings and conclusions Price support programs and crop insurance are substitutes in reducing producer risk because the availability of crop insurance led to little change in farm viability if price supports were available. Moreover, the availability of crop insurance in a setting with price supports allows producers to service higher levels of debt with no increase in risk.
Heimlich, Ralph. "Agricultural Programs and Cropland Conversion, 1975-1981," *Land Economics*, vol. 62, no. 2 (May 1986), 174- 181.	To examine the implications of legislation to reduce the conversion of rangeland and other land to cropland.	1986	For some newly converted highly erodible cropland, price support and farm credit program subsidies would make the difference between crop production revenues and variable costs positive. Farm programs would provide a subsidy for conversion of highly erodible land to cropland, averaging about $17 per acre.

Source: GAO's analysis of the studies cited.

REFERENCES

[1] According to U.S. Department of Agriculture's (USDA) National Resources Inventory, cropland includes areas used for the production of adapted crops for harvest; rangeland is composed principally of native grasses or other native vegetation suitable for grazing; and pastureland is land that is managed for introduced forage plants for grazing. The USDA definitions of cropland, rangeland, and pastureland are discussed in appendix II. For the purposes of this report, native grassland generally refers to rangeland unless otherwise specified.

[2] GAO, *Suggested Areas for Oversight for the 110th Congress*, GAO-07-235R (Washington, D.C.: Nov. 17, 2006).

[3] The marketing assistance loan program provides benefits to producers of major crops when market prices are low. We did not analyze the cost of marketing assistance loan payments. According to spending forecasts, marketing assistance loan payments are predicted to be zero for corn, soybeans, and wheat through 2011 because prices of these crops are expected to be above the levels that trigger payments.

[4] Producers who grow a crop that is currently ineligible for crop insurance may be eligible for a direct payment under USDA's Farm Service Agency's Noninsured Assistance Program.

[5] Producers receive indemnity payments if they realize a qualifying crop loss under the crop insurance program.

[6] Pub. L. No. 110-28, tit. IX, § 9001, 121 Stat. 112 (2007).

[7] Pub. L. No. 99-198, 99 Stat. 1354 (1985) (codified as amended in scattered sections of titles 7 and 16 of U.S.C.).

[8] The cropland must have been converted for use in producing annually tilled agricultural commodity crops in order to come under the protections provided by Sodbuster.

[9] A conservation system is a combination of one or more conservation practices that are approved by NRCS. These practices include structural measures, such as terraces, or management techniques, such as conservation tillage, used to enhance, protect, or manage natural resources, including soil.

[10] All NRI numbers in this report are statistical estimates.

[11] FSA state officials in these states instructed county offices on the procedures to use in collecting data on conversions of grassland that had no cropping history to cropland, and they believe county offices used consistent procedures. However, they have not confirmed that the county offices used these procedures. As a result, some counties may have overreported or underreported the number of acres converted. In addition, it is possible that some of the converted land identified as previously uncropped grassland had been converted to cropland before FSA began keeping crop history records, was later returned to grassland, and then was again converted to cropland.

[12] Scott Stephens, Johanna Walker, Darin Blunck, Aneetha Jayaraman, and Dave Naugle, *Grassland Conversion in the Missouri Coteau of North and South Dakota 1984-2003*, Ducks Unlimited (forthcoming). Information from this report was presented as "Grassland Conversion and Risk Models for the Missouri Coteau: Tools for Staying Ahead of the Plow," at the annual conference of the South Dakota Wildlife Society, Oacoma, South Dakota, March, 2007.

[13] These counties are in a contiguous area that runs from southwest to northeast across Nebraska. NRCS officials believed conversion rates were relatively high in the counties of this area. According to FSA and NRCS officials in Nebraska, producers almost always carry out these planned conversions.

[14] We selected South Dakota counties because conversion data were available by county for 2005 and 2006 and conversions have received considerable attention in the state. In conducting this analysis, we assumed that the counties with the highest number of converted acres in 2005 and 2006 were also the counties with the highest conversion rates in previous years.

[15] In addition, we separated the 66 South Dakota counties into three groups based on the number of acres converted and found that the 22 counties with the highest number of converted acres had net crop

insurance benefits of about $600 million from 1997 to 2006, while the 22 counties with the lowest number of conversions had net benefits of about $100 million for the same time period.

[16] Crop disaster assistance payments are approved by the Congress on an ad hoc basis, and therefore these payments do not necessarily add to government costs every year. However, ad hoc crop disaster assistance payments have been available for nearly every crop year since 1988.

[17] GAO, Crop Insurance: Actions Needed to Reduce Program's Vulnerability to Fraud, Waste, and Abuse, GAO-05-528 (Washington, D.C.: Sept. 30, 2005).

[18] USDA Economic Research Service and Office of the Chief Economist, *An Analysis of the Effects of an Expansion in Biofuel Demand on U.S. Agriculture*, (Washington, D.C., May 2007).

[19] USDA National Agricultural Statistics Service, *Acreage*, June 29, 2007.

[20] To estimate crop prices for the 2007 crop enterprise, we used regional average crop prices for January to July 2007.

[21] Since this land had not been in crop production previously, under current legislation it would not be eligible for counter-cyclical payments or direct payments.

[22] The Wetlands Reserve Program was authorized by the Food, Agriculture, Conservation, and Trade Act of 1990 (1990 Farm Bill), Pub. L. No. 101-624, 104 Stat. 3359, to assist landowners in restoring and protecting wetlands. Producers enrolling in the program must agree to implement approved wetland restoration and protection plans. In return, participating producers receive payments based on the fair market value of the land covered by the easement. The 2002 Farm Bill reauthorized the program with mandatory funding through fiscal year 2007 and set a maximum enrollment ceiling of 2.275 million acres.

[23] The Grassland Reserve Program was authorized in the 2002 Farm Bill, which authorized enrollment of up to 2 million acres of restored or improved grassland, rangeland, and pastureland under temporary and permanent easements or rental agreements of at least 10 years. A total of $254 million in mandatory funding between fiscal years 2003 and 2007 was provided. The 2002 Farm Bill also provided cost sharing payments at 75 percent to restore disturbed grasslands and 90 percent to protect virgin grasslands.

[24] This survey was done in conjunction with our work on *Agricultural Conservation: USDA Needs to Better Ensure Protection of Highly Erodible Cropland and Wetlands*, GAO-03-418 (Washington, D.C.:

Apr. 21, 2003). See also the special publication, *Agricultural Conservation: Survey Results on USDA's Implementation of Food Security Act Compliance Provisions* (GAO-03-492SP, Apr. 21, 2003), which includes survey results stratified by state.

Appendix I

[1] The NRI, conducted by NRCS in cooperation with Iowa State University's Center for Survey Statistics and Methodology, is a statistical survey of land use and natural resource conditions and trends on U.S. nonfederal lands.

[2] NASS conducts yearly surveys to gather data on aspects of U.S. agriculture production. NASS also administers the Census of Agriculture, a comprehensive census of U.S. agriculture producers that is conducted every 5 years.

[3] Scott Stephens, Johanna Walker, Darin Blunck, Aneetha Jayaraman, and Dave Naugle. *Grassland Conversion in the Missouri Coteau of North and South Dakota 1984-2003*, Ducks Unlimited (forthcoming). Information from this report was presented as "Grassland Conversion and Risk Models for the Missouri Coteau: Tools for Staying Ahead of the Plow," at the annual conference of the South Dakota Wildlife Society, Oacoma, South Dakota, March, 2007.

[4] Richard Conner, Andrew Seidl, Larry Van Tassell, and Neal Wilkins, "United States Grasslands and Related Resources: An Economic and Biological Trends Assessment," a special report prepared with financial support from the National Cattlemen's Beef Association, The Nature Conservancy, and Ducks Unlimited, 2001.

[5] N. Ramankutty and J. E. Foley, "Estimating historical changes in land cover: North American croplands from 1850 to 1992," *Global Ecology and Biogeography*, 8: 381-396 (1999).

[6] To qualify for farm program payments, a producer must certify compliance with conservation provisions. To qualify under Sodbuster provisions, a producer seeking to convert previously uncropped land to cropland notifies FSA of that intention. FSA then requests a determination for highly erodible land. According to FSA and NRCS officials, after informing USDA of their intention to convert land, producers seldom decide not to carry out the conversion.

[7] This survey was conducted in conjunction with our work on GAO-03-418. Specifically, in September 2002, we surveyed staff—usually the

district conservationist—responsible for the conservation compliance reviews in each of NRCS's 2,549 field offices that conducted compliance reviews during the period 1998 through 2001 to obtain information on their understanding and implementation of conservation provisions, and their views on the effectiveness of these provisions.

Appendix II

[1] Rangeland is a USDA land cover/use category on which the plant cover is composed principally of native grasses, grasslike plants, forbs or shrubs suitable for grazing, and introduced forage species that are managed like rangeland, with little or no chemicals or fertilizer being applied. Grasslands, savannas, many wetlands, some deserts, and tundra are considered to be rangeland. Pastureland is a USDA land cover/use category of land managed primarily for the production of introduced forage plants for livestock grazing. Management of pastureland usually consists of treatments such as fertilization, weed control, reseeding or renovation, and control of grazing. Cropland is a USDA land cover/use category that includes areas used for the production of adapted crops for harvest. Two subcategories of cropland are recognized: cultivated and noncultivated. Cultivated land comprises land in row crops or close-grown crops and also other cultivated cropland, for example, hayland or pastureland that is in a rotation with row or close-grown crops. Noncultivated cropland includes permanent hayland and horticultural cropland.

Appendix III

[1] Between 1840 and 1996, the U.S. Department of Commerce, Bureau of the Census was responsible for collecting Census of Agriculture data. The Census of Agriculture Act, Pub. L. No. 105-113, 111 Stat. 2274 (1997), transferred the responsibility for the Census of Agriculture from the Bureau of the Census to the Secretary of Agriculture who subsequently delegated that responsibility to the Administrator of NASS.

[2] Idle cropland includes Conservation Reserve Program land unless the land was used for haying or grazing.

Appendix IV

[1] Michael D. Boehlje and Vernon R. Eidman, *Farm Management*, John Wiley and Sons, New York, 1984, pp. 237-242.

[2] Specifically, a partial budget analysis examines the additional returns that would result from adopting an alternative plan plus the decreased costs from no longer using a base plan, minus the sum of the additional costs of the alternative plan plus the reduced returns from the base plan. The partial budget only considers the direct private costs and benefits to the farmer and does not include the social costs and benefits to society that a change would bring about, such as to the environment or wildlife habitat.

[3] South Dakota State University, Department of Economics, Extension, Management Tools and Links, Livestock Budgets, Beef Cow Unit, Feeder Calf Sold, (B1CC). http://econ.sdstate.edu/Extension/Tools/budgets.htm.

[4] These rangeland production values are from the NRCS Web Soil Survey. www.websoilsurvey.nrcs.usda.gov/app/.

[5] *Drovers* is a monthly magazine and online livestock information service that provides business management and marketing information for all segments of the beef industry, including the female market, fed-cattle markets, and stocker/feeder prices.

[6] These "other costs," such as veterinary and medicine, were obtained from a South Dakota State University Extension area farm management specialist.

[7] Also, since the 2007 crop has not been harvested, we assumed a 3-year moving average county yield from NASS statistics, adjusted by expert opinion from our interviews with South Dakota soil scientists.

[8] Per our discussions with NRCS officials concerning Hand County, South Dakota, the soil types most likely to be converted were: ErB (Eakin-Raber Complex-Undulating), HkB (Houdek-Prosper Loams, Undulating), RaB (Raber Loams, Undulating), ReB (Raber-Eakin Complex, Undulating), WmB (Glenham Loam, Undulating), WpB (Glenham-Cavo, Undulating), and WzC (Glenham-Java, Rolling).

[9] For the cost estimates, we assumed that the cropping enterprise used no-till treatment rather than conventional tillage.

[10] Land newly converted into cropland would only qualify for marketing assistance benefits, such as loan deficiency payments, and would not be eligible for countercyclical payments or direct payments since the land would not have a cropping history.

[11] May 2007 supplemental appropriation legislation authorized crop disaster assistance payments for crop years 2005, 2006, and early 2007. Producers can receive a disaster assistance payment for only one of the 3 years. Because these payments had not been made as of July 2007, we did not include estimates of them in our analysis.

[12] Crop disaster assistance payments, which likely will be made for the 2006 crop year, are not included in this analysis.

[13] USDA Agricultural Projections to 2016, Interagency Agricultural Projections Committee, Long Term Projections Report OCE-2007-1, (Washington, D.C., February 2007).

INDEX

D

E

Y